WHAT'S WRONG
WITH THE WORLD

WHAT'S WRONG WITH THE WORLD

G. K. CHESTERTON

Sherwood Sugden & Company
PUBLISHERS
315 5th Street, Peru, Illinois 61354

ISBN 0-89385-037-3

Printed in the United States of America

Cover: From a photograph by Howard Coster.

DEDICATION

To C. F. G. MASTERMAN, M.P.

MY DEAR CHARLES,

I originally called this book "What is Wrong," and it would have satisfied your sardonic temper to note the number of social misunderstandings that arose from the use of the title. Many a mild lady visitor opened her eyes when I remarked casually, "I have been doing 'What is Wrong' all this morning." And one minister of religion moved quite sharply in his chair when I told him (as he understood it) that I had to run upstairs and do what was wrong, but should be down again in a minute. Exactly of what occult vice they silently accused me I cannot conjecture, but I know of what I accuse myself; and that is, of having written a very shapeless and inadequate book, and one quite unworthy to be dedicated to you. As far as literature goes, this book is what is wrong, and no mistake.

It may seem a refinement of insolence to present so wild a composition to one who has recorded two or three of the really impressive visions of the moving millions of England. You are the only man alive who can make the map of England crawl with life; a most creepy and enviable accomplishment. Why then should I trouble you with a book which, even if it achieves its object (which is monstrously unlikely), can only be a thundering gallop of theory?

Well, I do it partly because I think you politicians are none the worse for a few inconvenient ideals; but more because you will recognise the many arguments we have had; those arguments which the most wonderful ladies in the world can never endure for very long. And, perhaps, you will agree with me that the thread of comradeship and conversation must be protected because it is so frivolous. It must be held sacred, it must not be snapped, because it is not worth tying together again. It is exactly because argument is idle that men (I mean males) must take it seriously; for when (we feel), until the crack of doom, shall we have so delightful a difference again? But most of all I offer it to you because there exists not only comradeship, but a very different thing, called friendship; an agreement under all the arguments and a thread which, please God, will never break.

Yours always,

G. K. CHESTERTON.

CONTENTS

PAGE

PART I.—THE HOMELESSNESS OF MAN

  1. THE MEDICAL MISTAKE   3
  2. WANTED, AN UNPRACTICAL MAN   7
  3. THE NEW HYPOCRITE   13
  4. THE FEAR OF THE PAST   19
  5. THE UNFINISHED TEMPLE   27
  6. THE ENEMIES OF PROPERTY   33
  7. THE FREE FAMILY   37
  8. THE WILDNESS OF DOMESTICITY   42
  9. HISTORY OF HUDGE AND GUDGE   47
  10. OPPRESSION BY OPTIMISM   52
  11. THE HOMELESSNESS OF JONES   55

PART II.—IMPERIALISM: OR THE MISTAKE ABOUT MAN

  1. THE CHARM OF JINGOISM   61
  2. WISDOM AND THE WEATHER   65
  3. THE COMMON VISION   72
  4. THE INSANE NECESSITY   76

PART III.—FEMINISM: OR THE MISTAKE ABOUT WOMAN

  1. THE UNMILITARY SUFFRAGETTE   85
  2. THE UNIVERSAL STICK   88
  3. THE EMANCIPATION OF DOMESTICITY   95
  4. THE ROMANCE OF THRIFT   101
  5. THE COLDNESS OF CHLOE   107
  6. THE PEDANT AND THE SAVAGE   112

PART III. (*continued*)— PAGE

7. THE MODERN SURRENDER OF WOMAN   116
8. THE BRAND OF THE FLEUR DE LYS   119
9. SINCERITY AND THE GALLOWS   123
10. THE HIGHER ANARCHY   126
11. THE QUEEN AND THE SUFFRAGETTES   131
12. THE MODERN SLAVE   133

PART IV.—EDUCATION: OR THE MISTAKE ABOUT THE CHILD

1. THE CALVINISM OF TO-DAY   139
2. THE TRIBAL TERROR   142
3. THE TRICKS OF ENVIRONMENT   145
4. THE TRUTH ABOUT EDUCATION   147
5. AN EVIL CRY   150
6. AUTHORITY THE UNAVOIDABLE   153
7. THE HUMILITY OF MRS. GRUNDY   158
8. THE BROKEN RAINBOW   162
9. THE NEED FOR NARROWNESS   166
10. THE CASE FOR THE PUBLIC SCHOOLS   169
11. THE SCHOOL FOR HYPOCRITES   175
12. THE STALENESS OF THE NEW SCHOOLS   181
13. THE OUTLAWED PARENT   185
14. FOLLY AND FEMALE EDUCATION   189

PART V.—THE HOME OF MAN

1. THE EMPIRE OF THE INSECT   195
2. THE FALLACY OF THE UMBRELLA STAND   202
3. THE DREADFUL DUTY OF GUDGE   207
4. A DOUBT   210
5. CONCLUSION   212

PART I

THE HOMELESSNESS OF MAN

Chapter One

THE MEDICAL MISTAKE

A BOOK of modern social inquiry has a shape that is somewhat sharply defined. It begins as a rule with an analysis, with statistics, tables of population, decrease of crime among Congregationalists, growth of hysteria among policemen, and similar ascertained facts; it ends with a chapter that is generally called "The Remedy." It is almost wholly due to this careful, solid, and scientific method that "The Remedy" is never found. For this scheme of medical question and answer is a blunder; the first great blunder of sociology. It is always called stating the disease before we find the cure. But it is the whole definition and dignity of man that in social matters we must actually find the cure before we find the disease.

The fallacy is one of the fifty fallacies that come from the modern madness for biological or bodily metaphors. It is convenient to speak of the Social Organism, just as it is convenient to speak of the British Lion. But Britain is no more an organism than Britain is a lion. The moment we begin to give a nation the unity and simplicity of an animal, we begin to think wildly. Because every man is a biped, fifty men are not a centipede. This has produced, for instance, the

gaping absurdity of perpetually talking about "young nations" and "dying nations," as if a nation had a fixed and
physical span of life. Thus people will say that Spain has
entered a final senility; they might as well say that Spain
is losing all her teeth. Or people will say that Canada should
soon produce a literature; which is like saying that Canada
must soon grow a moustache. Nations consist of people; the
first generation may be decrepit, or the ten thousandth may
be vigorous. Similar applications of the fallacy are made by
those who see in the increasing size of national possessions,
a simple increase in wisdom and stature, and in favour with
God and man. These people, indeed, even fall short in
subtlety of the parallel of a human body. They do not even
ask whether an empire is growing taller in its youth, or only
growing fatter in its old age. But of all the instances of error
arising from this physical fancy, the worst is that we have
before us: the habit of exhaustively describing a social sick-
ness, and then propounding a social drug.

Now we do talk first about the disease in cases of bodily
breakdown; and that for an excellent reason. Because, though
there may be doubt about the way in which the body broke
down, there is no doubt at all about the shape in which it
should be built up again. No doctor proposes to produce a
new kind of man, with a new arrangement of eyes or limbs.
The hospital, by necessity, may send a man home with one
leg less: but it will not (in a creative rapture) send him home
with one leg extra. Medical science is content with the normal
human body, and only seeks to restore it.

But social science is by no means always content with the
normal human soul; it has all sorts of fancy souls for sale.
Man as a social idealist will say "I am tired of being a Puritan;
I want to be a Pagan," or "Beyond this dark probation of

Individualism I see the shining paradise of Collectivism."
Now in bodily ills there is none of this difference about the
ultimate ideal. The patient may or may not want quinine; but
he certainly wants health. No one says "I am tired of this
headache; I want some toothache," or "The only thing for this
Russian Influenza is a few German Measles," or "Through
this dark probation of catarrh I see the shining paradise of
rheumatism." But exactly the whole difficulty in our public
problems is that some men are aiming at cures which other
men would regard as worse maladies: are offering ultimate
conditions as states of health which others would uncompro-
misingly call states of disease. Mr. Belloc once said that he
would no more part with the idea of property than with his
teeth; yet to Mr. Bernard Shaw property is not a tooth, but
a toothache. Lord Milner has sincerely attempted to introduce German efficiency; and many of us would as soon wel-
come German Measles. Dr. Saleeby would honestly like to
have Eugenics; but I would rather have rheumatics.

This is the arresting and dominant fact about modern social
discussion; that the quarrel is not merely about the difficulties, but about the aim. We agree about the evil; it is about
the good that we should tear each other's eyes out. We all
admit that a lazy aristocracy is a bad thing. We should not
by any means all admit that an active aristocracy would be
a good thing. We all feel angry with an irreligious priesthood;
but some of us would go mad with disgust at a really religious one. Everyone is indignant if our army is weak, including the people who would be even more indignant if it
were strong. The social case is exactly the opposite of the
medical case. We do not disagree, like doctors, about the
precise nature of the illness, while agreeing about the nature
of health. On the contrary, we all agree that England is un-

healthy, but half of us would not look at her in what the other half would call blooming health. Public abuses are so prominent and pestilent that they sweep all generous people into a sort of fictitious unanimity. We forget that, while we agree about the abuses of things, we should differ very much about the uses of them. Mr. Cadbury and I would agree about the bad public-house. It would be precisely in front of the good public-house that our painful personal *fracas* would occur.

I maintain, therefore, that the common sociological method is quite useless: that of first dissecting abject poverty or cataloguing prostitution. We all dislike abject poverty; but it might be another business if we began to discuss independent and dignified poverty. We all disapprove of prostitution; but we do not all approve of purity. The only way to discuss the social evil is to get at once to the social ideal. We can all see the national madness; but what is national sanity? I have called this Book "What's Wrong with the World," but the rather wild title refers only to one point. What is wrong is that we do not ask what is right.

Chapter Two

WANTED, AN UNPRACTICAL MAN

THERE is a popular philosophical joke intended to typify the endless and useless arguments of philosophers; I mean the joke about which came first, the chicken or the egg. I am not sure that, properly understood, it is so futile an inquiry after all. I am not concerned here to enter on those deep metaphysical and theological differences of which the chicken and egg debate is a frivolous, but a very felicitous type. The evolutionary materialists are appropriately enough represented in the vision of all things coming from an egg, a dim and monstrous oval germ that got laid itself by accident. That other supernatural school of thought (to which I personally adhere) would be not unworthily typified in the fancy that this round world of ours is but an egg brooded upon by a sacred unbegotten bird—the mystic dove of the prophets. But it is to much humbler functions that I here call the awful power of such a distinction. Whether or no the living bird is at the beginning of our mental chain, it is absolutely necessary that it should be at the end of our mental chain. The bird is the thing to be aimed at—not with a gun, but a life-bestowing wand. What is essential to our right thinking is this: that the egg and the bird must not

be thought of as equal cosmic occurrences recurring alter-
nately for ever. They must not become a mere egg and bird
pattern, like the egg and dart pattern. One is a means and
the other an end; they are in different mental worlds. Leaving the complications of the human breakfast-table out of
account, in an elemental sense, the egg only exists to produce the chicken. But the chicken does not exist only in
order to produce another egg. He may also exist to amuse
himself, to praise God, and even to suggest ideas to a French
dramatist. Being a conscious life, he is, or may be, valuable
in himself. Now our modern politics are full of a noisy forgetfulness; forgetfulness that the production of this happy and
conscious life is after all the aim of all complexities and
compromises. We talk of nothing but useful men and working institutions; that is, we only think of the chickens as
things that will lay more eggs. Instead of seeking to breed
our ideal bird, the eagle of Zeus or the Swan of Avon, or
whatever we happen to want, we talk entirely in terms of
the process and the embryo. The process itself, divorced
from its divine object, becomes doubtful and even morbid;
poison enters the embryo of everything; and our politics are
rotten eggs.

Idealism is only considering everything in its practical
essence. Idealism only means that we should consider a
poker in reference to poking before we discuss its suitability
for wife-beating; that we should ask if an egg is good enough
for practical poultry-rearing before we decide that the egg
is bad enough for practical politics. But I know that this primary pursuit of the theory (which is but pursuit of the
aim) exposes one to the cheap charge of fiddling while
Rome is burning. A school, of which Lord Rosebery is representative, has endeavoured to substitute for the moral or
social ideals which have hitherto been the motives of politics

a general coherency or completeness in the social system which has gained the nickname of "efficiency." I am not very certain of the secret doctrine of this sect in the matter. But, as far as I can make out, "efficiency" means that we ought to discover everything about a machine except what it is for. There has arisen in our time a most singular fancy—the fancy that when things go very wrong we need a practical man. It would be far truer to say, that when things go very wrong we need an unpractical man. Certainly, at least, we need a theorist. A practical man means a man accustomed to mere daily practice, to the way things commonly work. When things will not work, you must have the thinker, the man who has some doctrine about why they work at all. It is wrong to fiddle while Rome is burning; but it is quite right to study the theory of hydraulics while Rome is burning.

It is then necessary to drop one's daily agnosticism and attempt *rerum cognoscere causas*. If your aeroplane has a slight indisposition, a handy man may mend it. But, if it is seriously ill, it is all the more likely that some absent-minded old Professor with wild white hair will have to be dragged out of a college or a laboratory to analyse the evil. The more complicated the smash, the whiter-haired and more absent-minded will be the theorist who is needed to deal with it; and in some extreme cases, no one but the man (probably insane) who invented your flying-ship could possibly say what was the matter with it.

"Efficiency," of course, is futile for the same reason that "strong men," "will power" and the superman are futile. That is, it is futile because it only deals with actions after they have been performed. It has no philosophy for incidents before they happen; therefore it has no power of choice. An act can only be successful or unsuccessful when it is over; if it is to begin it must be, in the abstract, right or wrong.

There is no such thing as backing a winner; for he cannot be a winner when he is backed. There is no such thing as fighting on the winning side; one fights to find out which is the winning side. If any operation has occurred, that operation was efficient. If a man is murdered, the murder was efficient. A tropical sun is as efficient in making people lazy as a Lancashire foreman bully in making them energetic. Maeterlinck is as efficient in filling a man with strange spiritual tremors as Messrs. Crosse and Blackwell are in filling a man with jam. But it all depends on what you want to be filled with. Lord Rosebery, being a modern sceptic, probably prefers the spiritual tremors. I, being an orthodox Christian, prefer the jam. But both are efficient when they have been effected; and inefficient until they are effected. A man who thinks much about success must be the drowsiest sentimentalist; for he must be always looking back. If he only likes victory he must always come late for the battle. For the man of action there is nothing but idealism.

This definite ideal is a far more urgent and practical matter in our existing English trouble than any immediate plans or proposals. For the present chaos is due to a sort of general oblivion of all that men were originally aiming at. No man demands what he desires; each man demands what he fancies he can get. Soon people forget what the man really wanted first; and after a successful and vigorous political life, he forgets it himself. The whole is an extravagant riot of second bests, a pandemonium of *pis-aller*. Now this sort of pliability does not merely prevent any heroic consistency; it also prevents any really practical compromise. One can only find the middle distance between two points if the two points will stand still. We may make an arrangement between two litigants who cannot both get what they want; but not if they will not even tell us what they want. The keeper of a restaurant would much prefer that each customer should give his order smartly, though it were for stewed ibis or boiled elephant, rather than that each customer should sit holding his head in his hands, plunged in arithmetical calculations about how much food there can be on the premises. Most of us have suffered from a certain sort of ladies who, by their perverse unselfishness, give more trouble than the selfish; who almost clamour for the unpopular dish and scramble for the worst seat. Most of us have known parties or expeditions full of this seething fuss of self-effacement. From much meaner motives than those of such admirable women, our practical politicians keep things in the same confusion through the same doubt about their real demands. There is nothing that so much prevents a settlement as a tangle of small surrenders. We are bewildered on every side by politicians who are in favour of secular education, but think it hopeless to work for it; who desire total prohibition, but are certain they should not demand it; who regret compulsory education, but resignedly continue it; or who want peasant proprietorship and therefore vote for something else. It is this dazed and floundering opportunism that gets in the way of everything. If our statesmen were visionaries something practical might be done. If we asked for something in the abstract we might get something in the concrete. As it is, it is not only impossible to get what one wants, but it is impossible to get any part of it, because nobody can mark it out plainly like a map. That clear and even hard quality that there was in the old bargaining has wholly vanished. We forget that the word "compromise" contains, among other things, the rigid and ringing word "promise." Moderation is not vague; it is as definite as perfection. The middle point is as fixed as the extreme point.

If I am made to walk the plank by a pirate, it is vain for

me to offer, as a common-sense compromise, to walk along
the plank for a reasonable distance. It is exactly about the
reasonable distance that the pirate and I differ. There is an
exquisite mathematical split second at which the plank tips
up. My common sense ends just before that instant; the
pirate's common sense begins just beyond it. But the point
itself is as hard as any geometrical diagram; as abstract as
any theological dogma.

Chapter Three

THE NEW HYPOCRITE

But this new cloudy political cowardice has rendered useless the old English compromise. People have begun to be terrified of an improvement merely because it is complete. They call it utopian and revolutionary that anyone should really have his own way, or anything be really done, and done with. Compromise used to mean that half a loaf was better than no bread. Among modern statesmen it really seems to mean that half a loaf is better than a whole loaf.

As an instance to sharpen the argument, I take the one case of our everlasting Education Bills. We have actually contrived to invent a new kind of hypocrite. The old hypocrite, Tartuffe or Pecksniff, was a man whose aims were really worldly and practical, while he pretended that they were religious. The new hypocrite is one whose aims are really religious, while he pretends that they are worldly and practical. The Rev. Brown, the Wesleyan minister, sturdily declares that he cares nothing for creeds, but only for education; meanwhile, in truth, the wildest Wesleyanism is tearing his soul. The Rev. Smith, of the Church of England, explains gracefully, with the Oxford manner, that the only question for him is the prosperity and efficiency of the schools; while in truth all the evil passions of a curate are roaring within him. It is a fight of creeds masquerading as policies. I think these reverend gentlemen do themselves wrong; I think they are more pious than they will admit. Theology is not (as some suppose) expunged as an error. It is merely concealed, like a sin. Dr. Clifford really wants a theological atmosphere as much as Lord Halifax; only it is a different one. If Dr. Clifford would ask plainly for Puritanism and Lord Halifax ask plainly for Catholicism, something might be done for them. We are all, one hopes, imaginative enough to recognise the dignity and distinctness of another religion, like Islam or the cult of Apollo. I am quite ready to respect another man's faith; but it is too much to ask that I should respect his doubt, his worldly hesitations and fictions, his political bargain and makebelieve. Most Nonconformists with an instinct for English history could see something poetic and national about the Archbishop of Canterbury as an Archbishop of Canterbury. It is when he does the rational British statesman that they very justifiably get annoyed. Most Anglicans with an eye for pluck and simplicity could admire Dr. Clifford as a Baptist minister. It is when he says that he is simply a citizen that nobody can possibly believe him.

But indeed the case is yet more curious than this. The one argument that used to be urged for our creedless vagueness was that at least it saved us from fanaticism. But it does not even do that. On the contrary it creates and renews fanaticism with a force quite peculiar to itself. This is at once so strange and so true that I will ask the reader's attention to it with a little more precision.

Some people do not like the word "dogma." Fortunately they are free, and there is an alternative for them. There are two things, and two things only, for the human mind, a dogma and a prejudice. The Middle Ages were a rational epoch, an age of doctrine. Our age is, at its best, a poetical epoch, an age of prejudice. A doctrine is a definite point; a prejudice is a direction. That an ox may be eaten, while a man should not be eaten, is a doctrine. That as little as possible of anything should be eaten is a prejudice; which is also sometimes called an ideal. Now a direction is always far more fantastic than a plan. I would rather have the most archaic map of the road to Brighton than a general recommendation to turn to the left. Straight lines that are not parallel must meet at last; but curves may recoil for ever. A pair of lovers might walk along the frontier of France and Germany, one on the one side and one on the other, so long as they were not vaguely told to keep away from each other. And this is a strictly true parable of the effect of our modern vagueness in losing and separating men as in a mist.

It is not merely true that a creed unites men. Nay, a difference of creed unites men—so long as it is a clear difference. A boundary unites. Many a magnanimous Moslem and chivalrous Crusader must have been much nearer to each other, because they were both dogmatists, than any two homeless agnostics in a pew of Mr. Campbell's chapel. "I say God is One," and "I say God is One but also Three," that is the beginning of a good quarrelsome, manly friendship. But our age would turn these creeds into tendencies. It would tell the Trinitarian to follow multiplicity as such (because it was his "temperament"), and he would turn up later with three hundred and thirty-three persons in the Trinity. Meanwhile, it would turn the Moslem into a Monist: a frightful intellectual fall. It would force that previously healthy person not only to admit that there was one God, but to admit that there was nobody else. When each had, for a long enough period, followed the gleam of his own nose (like the Dong) they would appear again; the Christian a Polytheist, and the Moslem a Panegoist, both quite mad, and far more unfit to understand each other than before.

It is exactly the same with politics. Our political vagueness divides men, it does not fuse them. Men will walk along the edge of a chasm in clear weather; but they will edge miles away from it in a fog. So a Tory can walk up to the very edge of Socialism, *if he knows what is Socialism*. But if he is told that Socialism is a spirit, a sublime atmosphere, a noble, indefinable tendency, why, then he keeps out of its way; and quite right too. One can meet an assertion with an argument; but healthy bigotry is the only way in which one can meet a tendency. I am told that the Japanese method of wrestling consists not of suddenly pressing, but of suddenly giving way. This is one of my many reasons for disliking the Japanese civilisation. To use surrender as a weapon is the very worst spirit of the East. But certainly there is no force so hard to fight as the force which it is easy to conquer; the force that always yields and then returns. Such is the force of a great impersonal prejudice, such as possesses the modern world on so many points. Against this there is no weapon at all except a rigid and steely sanity, a resolution not to listen to fads, and not to be infected by diseases.

In short, the rational human faith must armour itself with prejudice in an age of prejudices, just as it armoured itself with logic in an age of logic. But the difference between the two mental methods is marked and unmistakable. The essential of the difference is this: that prejudices are divergent, whereas creeds are always in collision. Believers bump into each other; whereas bigots keep out of each other's way. A creed is a collective thing, and even its sins are sociable. A prejudice is a private thing, and even its tolerance is misanthropic. So it is with our existing opinions. They keep out of each other's way; the Tory paper and the Radical paper do not answer each other; they ignore each other. Genuine controversy, fair cut and thrust before a common audience, has become in our special epoch very rare. For the sincere controversialist is above all things a good listener. The really burning enthusiast never interrupts; he listens to the enemy's arguments as eagerly as a spy would listen to the enemy's arrangements. But if you attempt an actual argument with a modern paper of opposite politics, you will find that no medium is admitted between violence and evasion. You will have no answer except slanging or silence. A modern editor must not have that eager ear that goes with the honest tongue. He may be deaf and silent; and that is called dignity. Or he may be deaf and noisy; and that is called slashing journalism. In neither case is there any controversy; for the whole object of modern party combatants is to charge out of earshot.

The only logical cure for all this is the assertion of a human ideal. In dealing with this, I will try to be as little transcendental as is consistent with reason; it is enough to say that unless we have some doctrine of a divine man, all abuses may be excused, since evolution may turn them into uses. It will be easy for the scientific plutocrat to maintain that humanity will adapt itself to any conditions which we now consider evil. The old tyrants invoked the past; the new tyrants will invoke the future. Evolution has produced the snail and the owl; evolution can produce a workman who wants no more space than a snail, and no more light than an owl. The employer need not mind sending a Kaffir to work underground; he will soon become an underground animal, like a mole. He need not mind sending a diver to hold his breath

in the deep seas; he will soon be a deep-sea animal. Men
need not trouble to alter conditions; conditions will so soon
alter men. The head can be beaten small enough to fit the
hat. Do not knock the fetters off the slave; knock the slave
until he forgets the fetters. To all this plausible modern argument for oppression, the only adequate answer is, that there
is a permanent human ideal that must not be either confused or destroyed. The most important man on earth is the
perfect man who is not there. The Christian religion has
specially uttered the ultimate sanity of our souls by maintaining this idea of the incarnate and human truth. Our
lives and laws are not judged by divine superiority, but
simply by human perfection. It is man, says Aristotle, who
is the measure. It is the Son of Man, says Scripture, who shall
judge the quick and the dead.

Doctrine, therefore, does not cause dissensions; rather a
doctrine alone can cure our dissensions. It is necessary to
ask, however roughly, what abstract and ideal shape in state
or family would fulfil the human hunger; and this apart
from whether we can completely obtain it or not. But when
we come to ask what is the need of normal men, what is
the desire of all nations, what is the ideal house, or road, or
rule, or republic, or king, or priesthood, then we are confronted with a strange and irritating difficulty peculiar to
the present time; and we must call a temporary halt and
examine that obstacle.

Chapter Four

THE FEAR OF THE PAST

THE last few decades have been marked by a special cultivation of the romance of the future. We seem to have made up our minds to misunderstand what has happened; and we turn, with a sort of relief, to stating what will happen—which is (apparently) much easier. The modern man no longer preserves the memoirs of his great-grandfather; but he is engaged in writing a detailed and authoritative biography of his great-grandson. Instead of trembling before the spectres of the dead, we shudder abjectly under the shadow of the babe unborn. This spirit is apparent everywhere, even to the creation of a form of futurist romance. Sir Walter Scott stands at the dawn of the nineteenth century for the novel of the past; Mr. H. G. Wells stands at the dawn of the twentieth century for the novel of the future. The old story, we know, was supposed to begin: "Late on a winter's evening two horsemen might have been seen——." The new story has to begin: "Late on a winter's evening two aviators will be seen——." The movement is not without its elements of charm; there is something spirited, if eccentric, in the sight of so many people fighting over again the fights that have not yet happened; of people still glowing with the memory of to-morrow morning. A man in advance of the age is a familiar phrase enough. An age in advance of the age is really rather odd.

But when full allowance has been made for this harmless element of poetry and pretty human perversity in the thing, I shall not hesitate to maintain here that this cult of the future is not only a weakness but a cowardice of the age. It is the peculiar evil of this epoch that even its pugnacity is fundamentally frightened; and the Jingo is contemptible not because he is impudent, but because he is timid. The reason why modern armaments do not inflame the imagination like the arms and emblazonments of the Crusades is a reason quite apart from optical ugliness or beauty. Some battleships are as beautiful as the sea; and many Norman nosepieces were as ugly as Norman noses. The atmospheric ugliness that surrounds our scientific war is an emanation from that evil panic which is at the heart of it. The charge of the Crusades was a charge; it was charging towards God, the wild consolation of the brave. The charge of the modern armaments is not a charge at all. It is a rout, a retreat, a flight from the devil, who will catch the hindmost. It is impossible to imagine a mediæval knight talking of longer and longer French lances, with precisely the quivering intonation employed about larger and larger German ships. The man who called the Blue Water School the "Blue Funk School" uttered a psychological truth which that school itself would scarcely essentially deny. Even the two-power standard, if it be a necessity, is in a sense a degrading necessity. Nothing has more alienated many magnanimous minds from Imperial enterprises than the fact that they are always exhibited as stealthy or sudden defences against a world of cold rapacity and fear. The Boer War, for instance, was coloured not so much by the creed that we were doing something right, as by the creed that Boers and Germans were probably doing something wrong; driving us (as it was said) to the sea. Mr. Chamberlain, I think, said that the war was a feather in his cap; and so it was: a white feather.

Now this same primary panic that I feel in our rush towards patriotic armaments I feel also in our rush towards future visions of society. The modern mind is forced towards the future by a certain sense of fatigue, not unmixed with terror, with which it regards the past. It is propelled towards the coming time; it is, in the exact words of the popular phrase, knocked into the middle of next week. And the goad which drives it on thus eagerly is not an affection for futurity. Futurity does not exist, because it is still future. Rather it is a fear of the past; a fear not merely of the evil in the past, but of the good in the past also. The brain breaks down under the unbearable virtue of mankind. There have been so many flaming faiths that we cannot hold; so many harsh heroisms that we cannot imitate; so many great efforts of monumental building or of military glory which seem to us at once sublime and pathetic. The future is a refuge from the fierce competition of our forefathers. The older generation, not the younger, is knocking at our door. It is agreeable to escape, as Henley said, into the Street of By-and-Bye, where stands the Hostelry of Never. It is pleasant to play with children, especially unborn children. The future is a blank wall on which every man can write his own name as large as he likes; the past I find already covered with illegible scribbles, such as Plato, Isaiah, Shakespeare, Michael Angelo, Napoleon. I can make the future as narrow as myself; the past is obliged to be as broad and turbulent as humanity. And the upshot of this modern attitude is really this: that men invent new ideals because they dare not at-

tempt old ideals. They look forward with enthusiasm, because they are afraid to look back.

Now in history there is no Revolution that is not a Restoration. Among the many things that leave me doubtful about
the modern habit of fixing eyes on the future, none is
stronger than this: that all the men in history who have really
done anything with the future have had their eyes fixed
upon the past. I need not mention the Renaissance, the very
word proves my case. The originality of Michael Angelo
and Shakespeare began with the digging up of old vases
and manuscripts. The wildness of poets absolutely arose out
of the mildness of antiquaries. So the great mediæval revival
was a memory of the Roman Empire. So the Reformation
looked back to the Bible and Bible times. So the modern
Catholic movement has looked back to patristic times. But
that modern movement which many would count the most
anarchic of all is in this sense the most conservative of all.
Never was the past more venerated by men than it was by
the French Revolutionists. They invoked the little republics
of antiquity with the complete confidence of one who in-
vokes the gods. The Sansculottes believed (as their name
might imply) in a return to simplicity. They believed most
piously in a remote past; some might call it a mythical past.
For some strange reason man must always thus plant his
fruit trees in a graveyard. Man can only find life among the
dead. Man is a misshapen monster, with his feet set forward
and his face turned back. He can make the future luxuriant
and gigantic, so long as he is thinking about the past. When
he tries to think about the future itself his mind diminishes
to a pin point with imbecility, which some call Nirvana.
To-morrow is the Gorgon; a man must only see it mirrored
in the shining shield of yesterday. If he sees it directly he
is turned to stone. This has been the fate of all those who

have really seen fate and futurity as clear and inevitable. The Calvinists, with their perfect creed of predestination, were turned to stone. The modern sociological scientists (with their excruciating Eugenics) are turned to stone. The only difference is that the Puritans make dignified, and the Eugenists somewhat amusing, statues.

But there is one feature in the past which more than all the rest defies and depresses the moderns and drives them toward this featureless future. I mean the presence in the past of huge ideals, unfulfilled and sometimes abandoned. The sight of these splendid failures is melancholy to a restless and rather morbid generation; and they maintain a strange silence about them—sometimes amounting to an unscrupulous silence. They keep them entirely out of their newspapers and almost entirely out of their history books. For example, they will often tell you (in their praises of the coming age) that we are moving on towards a United States of Europe. But they carefully omit to tell you that we are moving away from a United States of Europe; that such a thing existed literally in Roman and essentially in mediæval times. They never admit that the international hatreds (which they call barbaric) are really very recent, the mere breakdown of the ideal of the Holy Roman Empire. Or again, they will tell you that there is going to be a social revolution, a great rising of the poor against the rich; but they never rub it in that France made that magnificent attempt unaided, and that we and all the world allowed it to be trampled out and forgotten. I say decisively that nothing is so marked in modern writing as the prediction of such ideals in the future combined with the ignoring of them in the past. Anyone can test this for himself. Read any thirty or forty pages or pamphlets advocating peace in Europe, and see how many of them praise the old Popes or

Emperors for keeping the peace in Europe. Read any arm-
ful of essays and poems in praise of social democracy, and
see how many of them praise the old Jacobins who created
democracy and died for it. These colossal ruins are to the
modern only enormous eyesores. He looks back along the
valley of the past and sees a perspective of splendid but
unfinished cities. They are unfinished, not always through
enmity or accident, but often through fickleness, mental
fatigue, and the lust for alien philosophies. We have not
only left undone those things that we ought to have done;
but we have even left undone those things that we wanted
to do.

It is very currently suggested that the modern man is the
heir of all the ages, that he has got the good out of these
successive human experiments. I know not what to say in
answer to this, except to ask the reader to look at the modern man, as I have just looked at the modern man—in the
looking-glass. Is it really true that you and I are two starry
towers built up of all the most towering visions of the past?
Have we really fulfilled all the great historic ideals one after
the other, from our naked ancestor who was brave enough
to kill a mammoth with a stone knife, through the Greek
citizen and the Christian saint to our own grandfather or
great-grandfather, who may have been sabred by the Manchester Yeomanry or shot in the '48? Are we still strong
enough to spear mammoths, but now tender enough to spare
them? Does the cosmos contain any mammoth that we have
either speared or spared? When we decline (in a marked
manner) to fly the red flag and fire across a barricade like
our grandfathers, are we really declining in deference to
sociologists—or to soldiers? Have we indeed outstripped the
warrior and passed the ascetical saint? I fear we only out-
strip the warrior in the sense that we should probably run

away from him. And if we have passed the saint, I fear we have passed him without bowing.

This is, first and foremost, what I mean by the narrowness of the new ideas, the limiting effect of the future. Our modern prophetic idealism is narrow because it has undergone a persistent process of elimination. We must ask for new things because we are not allowed to ask for old things. The whole position is based on this idea that we have got all the good that can be got out of the ideas of the past. But we have not got all the good out of them, perhaps at this moment not any of the good out of them. And the need here is a need of complete freedom for restoration as well as revolution.

We often read nowadays of the valour or audacity with which some rebel attacks a hoary tyranny or an antiquated superstition. There is not really any courage at all in attacking hoary or antiquated things, any more than in offering to fight one's grandmother. The really courageous man is he who defies tyrannies young as the morning and superstitions fresh as the first flowers. The only true free-thinker is he whose intellect is as much free from the future as from the past. He cares as little for what will be as for what has been; he cares only for what ought to be. And for my present purpose I specially insist on this abstract independence. If I am to discuss what is wrong, one of the first things that are wrong is this: the deep and silent modern assumption that past things have become impossible. There is one metaphor of which the moderns are very fond; they are always saying, "You can't put the clock back." The simple and obvious answer is "You can." A clock, being a piece of human construction, can be restored by the human finger to any figure or hour. In the same way society, being a piece of human construction, can be reconstructed upon any plan that has ever existed.

There is another proverb, "As you have made your bed, so you must lie on it"; which again is simply a lie. If I have made my bed uncomfortable, please God I will make it again. We could restore the Heptarchy or the stage coaches if we chose. It might take some time to do, and it might be very inadvisable to do it; but certainly it is not impossible as bringing back last Friday is impossible. This is, as I say, the first freedom that I claim: the freedom to restore. I claim a right to propose as a solution the old patriarchal system of a Highland clan, if that should seem to eliminate the largest number of evils. It certainly would eliminate some evils; for instance, the unnatural sense of obeying cold and harsh strangers, mere bureaucrats and policemen. I claim the right to propose the complete independence of the small Greek or Italian towns, a sovereign city of Brixton or Brompton, if that seems the best way out of our troubles. It would be a way out of some of our troubles; we could not have in a small state, for instance, those enormous illusions about men or measures which are nourished by the great national or international newspapers. You could not persuade a city state that Mr. Beit was an Englishman, or Mr. Dillon a desperado, any more than you could persuade a Hampshire village that the village drunkard was a teetotaler or the village idiot a statesman. Nevertheless, I do not as a fact propose that the Browns and the Smiths should be collected under separate tartans. Nor do I even propose that Clapham should declare its independence. I merely declare my independence. I merely claim my choice of all the tools in the universe; and I shall not admit that any of them are blunted merely because they have been used.

Chapter Five

THE UNFINISHED TEMPLE

THE task of modern idealists indeed is made much too easy for them by the fact that they are always taught that if a thing has been defeated it has been disproved. Logically, the case is quite clearly the other way. The lost causes are exactly those which might have saved the world. If a man says that the Young Pretender would have made England happy, it is hard to answer him. If anyone says that the Georges made England happy, I hope we all know what to answer. That which was prevented is always impregnable; and the only perfect King of England was he who was smothered. Exactly because Jacobitism failed we cannot call it a failure. Precisely because the Commune collapsed as a rebellion we cannot say that it collapsed as a system. But such outbursts were brief or incidental. Few people realise how many of the largest efforts, the facts that will fill history, were frustrated in their full design and come down to us as gigantic cripples. I have only space to allude to the two largest facts of modern history: the Catholic Church, and that modern growth rooted in the French Revolution.

When four knights scattered the blood and brains of St.

Thomas of Canterbury, it was not only a sign of anger but of a sort of black admiration. They wished for his blood, but they wished even more for his brains. Such a blow will remain for ever unintelligible unless we realise what the brains of St. Thomas were thinking about just before they were distributed over the floor. They were thinking about the great mediæval conception that the church is the judge of the world. Becket objected to a priest being tried even by the Lord Chief Justice. And his reason was simple: because the Lord Chief Justice was being tried by the priest. The judiciary was itself *sub judice*. The kings were themselves in the dock. The idea was to create an invisible kingdom, without armies or prisons, but with complete freedom to condemn publicly all the kingdoms of the earth. Whether such a supreme church would have cured society we cannot affirm definitely; because the church never was a supreme church. We only know that in England at any rate the princes conquered the saints. What the world wanted we see before us; and some of us call it a failure. But we cannot call what the church wanted a failure; simply because the church failed. Tracy struck a little too soon. England had not yet made the great Protestant discovery that the king can do no wrong. The king was whipped in the cathedral; a performance which I recommend to those who regret the unpopularity of church-going. But the discovery was made; and Henry VIII scattered Becket's bones as easily as Tracy had scattered his brains.

Of course, I mean that Catholicism was not tried; plenty of Catholics were tried, and found guilty. My point is that the world did not tire of the church's ideal, but of its reality. Monasteries were impugned not for the chastity of monks, but for the unchastity of monks. Christianity was unpopular not because of the humility, but of the arrogance of Christians. Certainly, if the church failed it was largely through the churchmen. But at the same time hostile elements had certainly begun to rend it long before it could have done its work. In the nature of things it needed a common scheme of life and thought in Europe. Yet the mediæval system began to be broken to pieces intellectually long before it showed the slightest hint of falling to pieces morally. The huge early heresies, like the Albigenses, had not the faintest excuse in moral superiority. And it is actually true that the Reformation began to tear Europe apart before the Catholic Church had had time to pull it together. The Prussians, for instance, were not converted to Christianity at all until quite close to the Reformation. The poor creatures hardly had time to become Catholics before they were told to become Protestants. This explains a great deal of their subsequent conduct. But I have only taken this as the first and most evident case of the general truth: that the great ideals of the past failed not by being outlived (which must mean over-lived) but by not being lived enough. Mankind has not passed through the Middle Ages. Rather mankind has retreated from the Middle Ages in reaction and rout. The Christian ideal has not been tried and found wanting. It has been found difficult; and left untried.

It is, of course, the same in the case of the French Revolution. A great part of our present perplexity arises from the fact that the French Revolution has half succeeded and half failed. In one sense, Valmy was the decisive battle of the West, and in another Trafalgar. We have, indeed, destroyed the largest territorial tyrannies, and created a free peasantry in almost all Christian countries except England; of which we shall say more anon. But representative government, the one universal relic, is a very poor fragment of the full republican idea. The theory of the French Revolution presupposed two things in government, things which it achieved at the time, but which it has certainly not bequeathed to its imitators in England, Germany, and America. The first of these was the idea of honourable poverty: that a statesman must be something of a stoic; the second was the idea of extreme publicity. Many imaginative English writers, including Carlyle, seem quite unable to imagine how it was that men like Robespierre and Marat were ardently admired. The best answer is that they were admired for being poor—poor when they might have been rich.

No one will pretend that this ideal exists at all in the *haute politique* of this country. Our national claim to political incorruptibility is actually based on exactly the opposite argument; it is based on the theory that wealthy men in assured positions will have no temptation to financial trickery. Whether the history of the English aristocracy, from the spoliation of the monasteries to the annexation of the mines, entirely supports this theory I am not now enquiring; but certainly it is our theory, that wealth will be a protection against political corruption. The English statesman is bribed not to be bribed. He is born with a silver spoon in his mouth, so that he may never afterwards be found with the silver spoons in his pocket. So strong is our faith in this protection by plutocracy, that we are more and more trusting our empire in the hands of families which inherit wealth without either blood or manners. Some of our political houses are parvenu by pedigree; they hand on vulgarity like a coat-of-arms. In the case of many a modern statesman to say that he is born with a silver spoon in his mouth is at once inadequate and excessive. He is born with a silver knife in his mouth. But all this only illustrates the English theory that poverty is perilous for a politician.

It will be the same if we compare the conditions that

have come about with the Revolution legend touching publicity. The old democratic doctrine was that the more light that was let in to all departments of State, the easier it was for a righteous indignation to move promptly against wrong. In other words, monarchs were to live in glass houses, that mobs might throw stones. Again, no admirer of existing English politics (if there is any admirer of existing English politics) will really pretend that this ideal of publicity is exhausted, or even attempted. Obviously public life grows more private every day. The French have, indeed, continued the tradition of revealing secrets and making scandals; hence they are more flagrant and palpable than we, not in sin, but in the confession of sin. The first trial of Dreyfus might have happened in England; it is exactly the second trial that would have been legally impossible. But, indeed, if we wish to realise how far we fall short of the original republican outline, the sharpest way to test it is to note how far we fall short even of the republican element in the older regime. Not only are we less democratic than Danton and Condorcet, but we are in many ways less democratic than Choiseuil and Marie Antoinette. The richest nobles before the revolt were needy middle-class people compared with our Rothschilds and Russells. And in the matter of publicity the old French monarchy was infinitely more democratic than any of the monarchies of to-day. Practically anybody who chose could walk into the palace and see the king playing with his children, or paring his nails. The people possessed the monarch, as the people possess Primrose Hill; that is they cannot move it, but they can sprawl all over it. The old French monarchy was founded on the excellent principle that a cat may look at a king. But nowadays a cat may not look at a king; unless it is a very tame cat. Even where the press is free for criticism it is only used for adulation. The substantial difference comes to something uncommonly like this. Eighteenth-century tyranny meant that you could say "The K— of Br——rd is a profligate." Twentieth-century liberty really means that you are allowed to say "The King of Brentford is a model family man."

But we have delayed the main argument too long for the parenthetical purpose of showing that the great democratic dream, like the great mediæval dream, has in a strict and practical sense been a dream unfulfilled. Whatever is the matter with modern England it is not that we have carried out too literally, or achieved with disappointing completeness, either the Catholicism of Becket or the equality of Marat. Now I have taken these two cases merely because they are typical of ten thousand other cases; the world is full of these unfulfilled ideals, these uncompleted temples. History does not consist of completed and crumbling ruins; rather it consists of half-built villas abandoned by a bankrupt builder. This world is more like an unfinished suburb than a deserted cemetery.

Chapter Six

THE ENEMIES OF PROPERTY

But it is for this especial reason that such an explanation is necessary on the very threshold of the definition of ideals. For owing to that historic fallacy with which I have just dealt, numbers of readers will expect me, when I propound an ideal, to propound a new ideal. Now I have no notion at all of propounding a new ideal. There is no new ideal imaginable by the madness of modern sophists which will be anything like so startling as fulfilling any one of the old ones. On the day that any copybook maxim is carried out there will be something like an earthquake for all nations. There is only one thing new that can be done under the sun; and that is to look at the sun. If you attempt it on a blue day in June, you will know why men do not look straight at their ideals. There is only one really startling thing to be done with the ideal, and that is to do it. It is to face the flaming logical fact, and its frightful consequences. Christ knew that it would be a more stunning thunderbolt to fulfil the law than to destroy it. It is true of both the cases I have quoted, and of every case. The pagans had always adored purity: Athene, Artemis, Vesta. It was when the virgin martyrs began defiantly to practise purity that they rent them with wild beasts and rolled them on red-hot coals. The world had always loved the notion of the poor man uppermost; it can be proved by every legend from Cinderella to Whittington, by every poem from the Magnificat to the Marseillaise. The kings went mad against France not because she idealised this ideal, but because she realised it. Joseph of Austria and Catherine of Russia quite agreed that the people should rule; what horrified them was that the people did. The French Revolution, therefore, is the type of all true revolutions, because its ideal was as old as the Old Adam, but its fulfilment almost as fresh, as miraculous, and as new as the New Jerusalem.

But in the modern world we are primarily confronted with the extraordinary spectacle of people turning to new ideals because they have not tried the old. Men have not got tired of Christianity; they have never found enough Christianity to get tired of. Men have never wearied of political justice; they have wearied of waiting for it.

Now, for the purpose of this book, I propose to take only one of these old ideals; but one that is perhaps the oldest. I take the principle of domesticity: the ideal house; the happy family, the holy family of history. For the moment it is only necessary to remark that it is like the church and like the republic, now chiefly assailed by those who have never known it, or by those who have failed to fulfil it. Numberless modern women have rebelled against domesticity in theory because they have never known it in practice. Hosts of the poor are driven to the workhouse without ever having known the house. Generally speaking, the cultured class is shrieking to be let out of the decent home, just as the working class is shouting to be let into it.

Now if we take this house or home as a test, we may very generally lay the simple spiritual foundations or the idea.

God is that which can make something out of nothing. Man (it may truly be said) is that which can make something out of anything. In other words, while the joy of God must be unlimited creation, the special joy of man is limited creation, the combination of creation with limits. Man's pleasure, therefore, is to possess conditions, but also to be partly possessed by them; to be half-controlled by the flute he plays or by the field he digs. The excitement is to get the utmost out of given conditions; the conditions will stretch, but not indefinitely. A man can write an immortal sonnet on an old envelope, or hack a hero out of a lump of rock. But hacking a sonnet out of rock would be a laborious business, and making a hero out of an envelope is almost out of the sphere of practical politics. This fruitful strife with limitations, when it concerns some airy entertainment of an educated class, goes by the name of Art. But the mass of men have neither time nor aptitude for the invention of invisible or abstract beauty. For the mass of men the idea of artistic creation can only be expressed by an idea unpopular in present discussions—the idea of property. The average man cannot cut clay into the shape of a man; but he can cut earth into the shape of a garden; and though he arranges it with red geraniums and blue potatoes in alternate straight lines, he is still an artist; because he has chosen. The average man cannot paint the sunset whose colours he admires; but he can paint his own house with what colour he chooses; and though he paints it pea green with pink spots, he is still an artist; because that is his choice. Property is merely the art of the democracy. It means that every man should have something that he can shape in his own image, as he is shaped in the image of Heaven. But because he is not God, but only a graven image of God, his self expression must deal with limits; properly with limits that are strict and even small.

I am well aware that the word "property" has been defiled in our time by the corruption of the great capitalists. One would think, to hear people talk, that the Rothschilds and the Rockefellers were on the side of property. But obviously they are the enemies of property; because they are the enemies of their own limitations. They do not want their own land; but other people's. When they remove their neighbour's landmark, they also remove their own. A man who loves a little triangular field ought to love it because it is triangular; anyone who destroys the shape, by giving him more land, is a thief who has stolen a triangle. A man with the true poetry of possession wishes to see the wall where his garden meets Smith's garden; the hedge where his farm touches Brown's. He cannot see the shape of his own land unless he sees the edges of his neighbour's. It is the negation of property that the Duke of Sutherland should have all the farms in one estate; just as it would be the negation of marriage if he had all our wives in one harem.

Chapter Seven

THE FREE FAMILY

As I have said, I propose to take only one central instance; I will take the institution called the private house or home; the shell and organ of the family. We will consider cosmic and political tendencies simply as they strike that ancient and unique roof. Very few words will suffice for all I have to say about the family itself. I leave alone the speculations about its animal origin and the details of its social reconstruction; I am concerned only with its palpable omnipresence. It is a necessity for mankind; it is (if you like to put it so) a trap for mankind. Only by the hypocritical ignoring of a huge fact can anyone contrive to talk of "free love" as if love were an episode like lighting a cigarette, or whistling a tune. Suppose whenever a man lit a cigarette, a towering genie arose from the rings of smoke and followed him everywhere as a huge slave. Suppose whenever a man whistled a tune he "drew an angel down" and had to walk about for ever with a seraph on a string. These catastrophic images are but faint parallels to the earthquake consequences that Nature has attached to sex; and it is perfectly plain at the beginning that a man cannot be a free lover; he is either a traitor or a tied man. The second element that creates the family

37

is that its consequences, though colossal, are gradual; the cigarette produces a baby giant, the song only an infant seraph. Thence arises the necessity for some prolonged system of co-operation; and thence arises the family in its full educational sense.

It may be said that this institution of the home is the one anarchist institution. That is to say, it is older than law, and stands outside the State. By its nature it is refreshed or corrupted by indefinable forces of custom or kinship. This is not to be understood as meaning that the State has no authority over families; that State authority is invoked and ought to be invoked in many abnormal cases. But in most normal cases of family joys and sorrows, the State has no mode of entry. It is not so much that the law should not interfere, as that the law cannot. Just as there are fields too far off for law, so there are fields too near; as a man may see the North Pole before he sees his own backbone. Small and near matters escape control at least as much as vast and remote ones; and the real pains and pleasures of the family form a strong instance of this. If a baby cries for the moon, the policeman cannot procure the moon—but neither can he stop the baby. Creatures so close to each other as a husband and wife, or a mother and children, have powers of making each other happy or miserable with which no public coercion can deal. If a marriage could be dissolved every morning it would not give back his night's rest to a man kept awake by a curtain lecture; and what is the good of giving a man a lot of power where he only wants a little peace? The child must depend on the most imperfect mother; the mother may be devoted to the most unworthy children; in such relations legal revenges are vain. Even in the abnormal cases where the law may operate this difficulty is constantly found; as many a bewildered magistrate knows.

He has to save children from starvation by taking away their breadwinner. And he often has to break a wife's heart, because her husband has already broken her head. The State has no tool delicate enough to deracinate the rooted habits and tangled affections of the family; the two sexes, whether happy or unhappy, are glued together too tightly for us to get the blade of a legal penknife in between them. The man and the woman are one flesh—yes, even when they are not one spirit. Man is on all fours. Upon this ancient and anarchic intimacy, types of government have little or no effect; it is happy or unhappy, by its own sexual wholesomeness and genial habit, under the republic of Switzerland or the despotism of Siam. Even a republic in Siam would not have done much towards freeing the Siamese Twins.

The problem is not in marriage, but in sex; and would be felt under the freest concubinage. Nevertheless, the overwhelming mass of mankind has not believed in freedom in this matter, but rather in a more or less lasting tie. Tribes and civilisations differ about the occasions on which we may loosen the bond, but they all agree that there is a bond to be loosened, not a mere universal detachment. For the purposes of this book I am not concerned to discuss that mystical view of marriage in which I myself believe: the great European tradition which has made marriage a sacrament. It is enough to say here that heathen and Christian alike have regarded marriage as a tie; a thing not normally to be sundered. Briefly, this human belief in a sexual bond rests on a principle of which the modern mind has made a very inadequate study. It is, perhaps, most nearly paralleled by the principle of the second wind in walking. The principle is this: that in everything worth having, even in every pleasure, there is a point of pain or tedium that must be survived, so that the pleasure may revive and endure. The joy of battle comes after the first fear of death; the joy of reading Virgil comes after the bore of learning him; the glow of the sea-bather comes after the icy shock of the sea bath; and the success of the marriage comes after the failure of the honeymoon. All human vows, laws, and contracts are so many ways of surviving with success this breaking point, this instant of potential surrender.

In everything on this earth that is worth doing, there is a stage when no one would do it, except for necessity or honour. It is then that the Institution upholds a man and helps him on to the firmer ground ahead. Whether this solid fact of human nature is sufficient to justify the sublime dedication of Christian marriage is quite another matter; it is amply sufficient to justify the general human feeling of marriage as a fixed thing, dissolution of which is a fault, or at least an ignominy. The essential element is not so much duration as security. Two people must be tied together in order to do themselves justice; for twenty minutes at a dance, or for twenty years in a marriage. In both cases the point is, that if a man is bored in the first five minutes he must go on and force himself to be happy. Coercion is a kind of encouragement; and anarchy (or what some call liberty) is essentially oppressive, because it is essentially discouraging. If we all floated in the air like bubbles, free to drift anywhere at any instant, the practical result would be that no one would have the courage to begin a conversation. It would be so embarrassing to start a sentence in a friendly whisper, and then have to shout the last half of it because the other party was floating away into the free and formless ether. The two must hold each other to do justice to each other. If Americans can be divorced for "incompatibility of temper" I cannot conceive why they are not all divorced. I have known many happy marriages, but never a compatible one. The whole aim of marriage is to fight through and survive the instant when incompatibility becomes unquestionable. For a man and a woman, as such, are incompatible.

Chapter Eight

THE WILDNESS OF DOMESTICITY

In the course of this crude study we shall have to touch on what is called the problem of poverty, especially the dehumanised poverty of modern industrialism. But in this primary matter of the ideal the difficulty is not the problem of poverty, but the problem of wealth. It is the special psychology of leisure and luxury that falsifies life. Some experience of modern movements of the sort called "advanced" has led me to the conviction that they generally repose upon some experience peculiar to the rich. It is so with that fallacy of free love of which I have already spoken; the idea of sexuality as a string of episodes. That implies a long holiday in which to get tired of one woman, and a motor car in which to wander looking for others; it also implies money for maintenances. An omnibus conductor has hardly time to love his own wife, let alone other people's wives. And the success with which nuptial estrangements are depicted in modern "problem plays" is due to the fact that there is only one thing that a drama cannot depict—that is a hard day's work. I could give many other instances of this plutocratic assumption behind progressive fads. For instance, there is a plutocratic assumption behind the phrase "Why should woman

42

be economically dependent upon man?" The answer is that among poor and practical people she isn't; except in the sense in which he is dependent upon her. A hunter has to tear his clothes; there must be somebody to mend them. A fisher has to catch fish; there must be somebody to cook them. It is surely quite clear that this modern notion that woman is a mere "pretty clinging parasite," "a plaything," etc., arose through the sombre contemplation of some rich banking family, in which the banker at least went to the city and pretended to do something, while the banker's wife went to the Park and did not pretend to do anything at all. A poor man and his wife are a business partnership. If one partner in a firm of publishers interviews the authors while the other interviews the clerks, is one of them economically dependent? Was Hodder a pretty parasite clinging to Stoughton? Was Marshall a mere plaything for Snelgrove?

But of all the modern notions generated by mere wealth the worst is this: the notion that domesticity is dull and tame. Inside the home (they say) is dead decorum and routine; outside is adventure and variety. This is indeed a rich man's opinion. The rich man knows that his own house moves on vast and soundless wheels of wealth: is run by regiments of servants, by a swift and silent ritual. On the other hand, every sort of vagabondage or romance is open to him in the streets outside. He has plenty of money and can afford to be a tramp. His wildest adventure will end in a restaurant, while the yokel's tamest adventure may end in a police-court. If he smashes a window he can pay for it; if he smashes a man he can pension him. He can (like the millionaire in the story) buy an hotel to get a glass of gin. And because he, the luxurious man, dictates the tone of nearly all "advanced" and "progressive" thought, we have almost forgotten what a home really means to the overwhelming millions of mankind.

For the truth is, that to the moderately poor the home is the only place of liberty. Nay, it is the only place of anarchy. It is the only spot on the earth where a man can alter arrangements suddenly, make an experiment or indulge in a whim. Everywhere else he goes he must accept the strict rules of the shop, inn, club, or museum that he happens to enter. He can eat his meals on the floor in his own house if he likes. I often do it myself; it gives a curious, childish, poetic, picnic feeling. There would be considerable trouble if I tried to do it in an A.B.C. tea-shop. A man can wear a dressing-gown and slippers in his house; while I am sure that this would not be permitted at the Savoy, though I never actually tested the point. If you go to a restaurant you must drink some of the wines on the wine list, all of them if you insist, but certainly some of them. But if you have a house and garden you can try to make hollyhock tea or convolvulus wine if you like. For a plain, hard-working man the home is not the one tame place in the world of adventure. It is the one wild place in the world of rules and set tasks. The home is the one place where he can put the carpet on the ceiling or the slates on the floor if he wants to. When a man spends every night staggering from bar to bar or from music-hall to music-hall, we say that he is living an irregular life. But he is not; he is living a highly regular life, under the dull, and often oppressive laws of such places. Sometimes he is not allowed even to sit down in the bars; and frequently he is not allowed to sing in the music-halls. Hotels may be defined as places where you are forced to dress; and theatres may be defined as places where you are forbidden to smoke. A man can only picnic at home.

Now I take, as I have said, this small human omnipotence,

this possession of a definite cell or chamber of liberty, as the working model for the present inquiry. Whether we can give every Englishman a free home of his own or not, at least we should desire it; and he desires it. For the moment we speak of what he wants, not of what he expects to get. He wants, for instance, a separate house; he does not want a semi-detached house. He may be forced in the commercial race to share one wall with another man. Similarly he might be forced in a three-legged race to share one leg with another man; but it is not so that he pictures himself in his dreams of elegance and liberty. Again, he does not desire a flat. He can eat and sleep and praise God in a flat; he can eat and sleep and praise God in a railway train. But a railway train is not a house; because it is a house on wheels. And a flat is not a house; because it is a house on stilts. An idea of earthy contact and foundation, as well as an idea of separation and independence, is a part of this instructive human picture.

I take, then, this one institution as a test. As every normal man desires a woman, and children born of a woman, every normal man desires a house of his own to put them into. He does not merely want a roof above him and a chair below him; he wants an objective and a visible kingdom; a fire at which he can cook what food he likes, a door he can open to what friends he chooses. This is the normal appetite of men; I do not say there are not exceptions. There may be saints above the need and philanthropists below it. Opalstein, now he is a duke, may have got used to more than this; and when he was a convict may have got used to less. But the normality of the thing is enormous. To give nearly everybody ordinary houses would please nearly everybody; that is what I assert without apology. Now in modern England (as you eagerly point out) it is very difficult to give nearly everybody houses. Quite so; I merely set up the *desideratum;* and ask the reader to leave it standing there while he turns with me to a consideration of what really happens in the social wars of our time.

Chapter Nine

HISTORY OF HUDGE AND GUDGE

THERE is, let us say, a certain filthy rookery in Hoxton, dripping with disease and honeycombed with crime and promiscuity. There are, let us say, two noble and courageous young men, of pure intentions and (if you prefer it) noble birth; let us call them Hudge and Gudge. Hudge, let us say, is of a bustling sort; he points out that the people must at all costs be got out of this den; he subscribes and collects money, but he finds (despite the large financial interests of the Hudges) that the thing will have to be done on the cheap if it is to be done on the spot. He therefore runs up a row of tall bare tenements like beehives; and soon has all the poor people bundled into their little brick cells, which are certainly better than their old quarters, in so far as they are weather proof, well ventilated and supplied with clean water. But Gudge has a more delicate nature. He feels a nameless something lacking in the little brick boxes; he raises numberless objections; he even assails the celebrated Hudge Report, with the Gudge Minority Report; and by the end of a year or so has come to telling Hudge heatedly that the people were much happier where they were before. As the people preserve in both places precisely the same air of dazed amiability, it is very difficult to find out which is right. But at least one might safely say that no people ever liked stench or starvation as such, but only some peculiar pleasures entangled with them. Not so feels the sensitive Gudge. Long before the final quarrel (Hudge *v.* Gudge and Another), Gudge has succeeded in persuading himself that slums and stinks are really very nice things; that the habit of sleeping fourteen in a room is what has made our England great; and that the smell of open drains is absolutely essential to the rearing of a viking breed.

But meanwhile, has there been no degeneration in Hudge? Alas, I fear there has. Those maniacally ugly buildings which he originally put up as unpretentious sheds barely to shelter human life, grow every day more and more lovely to his deluded eye. Things he would never have dreamed of defending, except as crude necessities, things like common kitchens or infamous asbestos stoves, begin to shine quite sacredly before him, merely because they reflect the wrath of Gudge. He maintains, with the aid of eager little books by Socialists, that man is really happier in a hive than in a house. The practical difficulty of keeping total strangers out of your bedroom he describes as Brotherhood; and the necessity for climbing twenty-three flights of cold stone stairs, I dare say he calls Effort. The net result of their philanthropic adventure is this; that one has come to defending indefensible slums and still more indefensible slum-landlords; while the other has come to treating as divine the sheds and pipes which he only meant as desperate. Gudge is now a corrupt and apoplectic old Tory in the Carlton Club; if you mention poverty to him he roars at you in a thick, hoarse voice something that is conjectured to be "Do 'em good!" Nor is Hudge more happy; for he is a lean vegetarian with a grey, pointed beard and an unnaturally easy smile, who goes about telling everybody that at last we shall all sleep in one universal bed-room; and he lives in a Garden City, like one forgotten of God.

Such is the lamentable history of Hudge and Gudge; which I merely introduce as a type of an endless and exasperating misunderstanding which is always occurring in modern England. To get men out of a rookery men are put into a tenement; and at the beginning the healthy human soul loathes them both. A man's first desire is to get away as far as possible from the rookery, even should his mad course lead him to a model dwelling. The second desire is, naturally, to get away from the model dwelling, even if it should lead a man back to the rookery. But I am neither a Hudgian nor a Gudgian; and I think the mistakes of these two famous and fascinating persons arose from one simple fact. They arose from the fact that neither Hudge nor Gudge had ever thought for an instant what sort of house a man might probably like for himself. In short, they did not begin with the ideal; and, therefore, were not practical politicians.

We may now return to the purpose of our awkward parenthesis about the praise of the future and the failures of the past. A house of his own being the obvious ideal for every man, we may now ask (taking this need as typical of all such needs) why he hasn't got it; and whether it is in any philosophical sense his own fault. Now, I think that in some philosophical sense it is his own fault; I think in a yet more philosophical sense it is the fault of his philosophy. And this is what I have now to attempt to explain.

Burke, a fine rhetorician, who rarely faced realities, said (I think) that an Englishman's house is his castle. This is honestly entertaining; for as it happens the Englishman is almost the only man in Europe whose house is not his castle. Nearly everywhere else exists the assumption of peasant

proprietorship; that a poor man may be a landlord, though
he is only lord of his own land. Making the landlord and
the tenant the same person has certain trivial advantages,
as that the tenant pays no rent, while the landlord does a
little work. But I am not concerned with the defence of small
proprietorship, but merely with the fact that it exists almost
everywhere except in England. It is also true, however, that
this estate of small possession is attacked everywhere to-day;
it has never existed among ourselves, and it may be destroyed among our neighbours. We have, therefore, to ask
ourselves what it is in human affairs generally, and in this
domestic ideal in particular, that has really ruined the natural human creation, especially in this country.

Man has always lost his way. He has been a tramp ever
since Eden; but he always knew, or thought he knew, what
he was looking for. Every man has a house somewhere in
the elaborate cosmos; his house waits for him waist deep in
slow Norfolk rivers or sunning itself upon Sussex downs.
Man has always been looking for that home which is the subject matter of this book. But in the bleak and blinding hail
of scepticism to which he has been now so long subjected, he
has begun for the first time to be chilled, not merely in his
hopes, but in his desires. For the first time in history he begins really to doubt the object of his wanderings on the
earth. He has always lost his way; but now he has lost his
address.

Under the pressure of certain upper class philosophies
(or in other words, under the pressure of Hudge and
Gudge) the average man has really become bewildered
about the goal of his efforts; and his efforts, therefore, grow
feebler and feebler. His simple notion of having a home of
his own is derided as bourgeois, as sentimental, or as despi-
cably Christian. Under various verbal forms he is recom-

mended to go on to the streets—which is called Individualism; or to the workhouse—which is called Collectivism. We
shall consider this process somewhat more carefully in a moment. But it may be said here that Hudge and Gudge, or
the governing class generally, will never fail for lack of some
modern phrase to cover their ancient predominance. The
great lords will refuse the English peasant his three acres
and a cow on advanced grounds, if they cannot refuse it
longer on reactionary grounds. They will deny him the three
acres on grounds of State Ownership. They will forbid him
the cow on grounds of humanitarianism.

And this brings us to the ultimate analysis of this singular influence that has prevented doctrinal demands by the
English people. There are, I believe, some who still deny
that England is governed by an oligarchy. It is quite enough
for me to know that a man might have gone to sleep some
thirty years ago over the day's newspaper and woken up
last week over the later newspaper, and fancied he was reading about the same people. In the one paper he would have
found a Lord Robert Cecil, a Mr. Gladstone, a Mr. Wyndham, a Churchill, a Chamberlain, a Trevelyan, a Buxton. In
the other paper he would find a Lord Robert Cecil, a Mr.
Gladstone, a Mr. Wyndham, a Churchill, a Chamberlain, a
Trevelyan, a Buxton. If this is not being governed by families
I cannot imagine what it is. I suppose it is being governed by
extraordinary democratic coincidences.

Chapter Ten

OPPRESSION BY OPTIMISM

But we are not here concerned with the nature and existence of the aristocracy, but with the origin of its peculiar power; why is it the last of the true oligarchies of Europe; and why does there seem no very immediate prospect of our seeing the end of it? The explanation is simple, though it remains strangely unnoticed. The friends of aristocracy often praise it for preserving ancient and gracious traditions. The enemies of aristocracy often blame it for clinging to cruel or antiquated customs. Both its enemies and its friends are wrong. Generally speaking the aristocracy does not preserve either good or bad traditions; it does not preserve anything except game. Who would dream of looking among aristocrats anywhere for an old custom? One might as well look for an old costume! The god of the aristocrats is not tradition, but fashion, which is the opposite of tradition. If you wanted to find an old-world Norwegian head-dress, would you look for it in the Scandinavian Smart Set? No; the aristocrats never have customs; at the best they have habits, like the animals. Only the mob has customs.

The real power of the English aristocrats has lain in exactly the opposite of tradition. The simple key to the power of our upper classes is this: that they have always kept carefully on the side of what is called Progress. They have al-

ways been up to date, and this comes quite easy to an aristocracy. For the aristocracy are the supreme instances of that
frame of mind of which we spoke just now. Novelty is to
them a luxury verging on a necessity. They, above all, are
so bored with the past and with the present, that they gape,
with a horrible hunger, for the future.

But whatever else the great lords forgot they never forgot
that it was their business to stand for the new things, for
whatever was being most talked about among university
dons or fussy financiers. Thus they were on the side of the
Reformation against the Church, of the Whigs against the
Stuarts, of the Baconian science against the old philosophy,
of the manufacturing system against the operatives, and
(to-day) of the increased power of the State against the
old-fashioned Individualists. In short, the rich are always
modern; it is their business. But the immediate effect of
this fact upon the question we are studying is somewhat
singular.

In each of the separate holes or quandaries in which the
ordinary Englishman has been placed, he has been told that
his situation is, for some particular reason, all for the best.
He woke up one fine morning and discovered that the public
things, which for eight hundred years he had used at once
as inns and sanctuaries, had all been suddenly and savagely
abolished, to increase the private wealth of about six or
seven men. One would think he might have been annoyed
at that; in many places he was and was put down by the
soldiery. But it was not merely the army that kept him
quiet. He was kept quiet by the sages as well as the soldiers;
the six or seven men who took away the inns of the poor told
him that they were not doing it for themselves, but for the
religion of the future, the great dawn of Protestantism and
truth. So whenever a seventeenth-century noble was caught

pulling down a peasant's fence and stealing his field, the noble pointed excitedly at the face of Charles I. or James II. (which at that moment, perhaps, wore a cross expression) and thus diverted the simple peasant's attention. The great Puritan lords created the Commonwealth, and destroyed the common land. They saved their poorer countrymen from the disgrace of paying Ship Money, by taking from them the plough money and spade money which they were doubtless too weak to guard. A fine old English rhyme has immortalised this easy aristocratic habit—

> You prosecute the man or woman
> Who steals the goose from off the common,
> But leave the larger felon loose
> Who steals the common from the goose.

But here, as in the case of the monasteries, we confront the strange problem of submission. If they stole the common from the goose, one can only say that he was a great goose to stand it. The truth is that they reasoned with the goose; they explained to him that all this was needed to get the Stuart fox over seas. So in the nineteenth century the great nobles who became mine-owners and railway directors, earnestly assured everybody that they did not do this from preference, but owing to a newly discovered Economic Law. So the prosperous politicians of our own generation introduce bills to prevent poor mothers from going about with their own babies; or they calmly forbid their tenants to drink beer in public inns. But this insolence is not (as you would suppose) howled at by everybody as outrageous feudalism. It is gently rebuked as Socialism. For an aristocracy is always progressive; it is a form of going the pace. Their parties grow later and later at night; for they are trying to live to-morrow.

Chapter Eleven

THE HOMELESSNESS OF JONES

THUS the Future of which we spoke at the beginning has (in England at least) always been the ally of tyranny. The ordinary Englishman has been duped out of his old possessions, such as they were, and always in the name of progress. The destroyers of the abbeys took away his bread and gave him a stone, assuring him that it was a precious stone, the white pebble of the Lord's elect. They took away his maypole and his original rural life and promised him instead the Golden Age of Peace and Commerce inaugurated at the Crystal Palace. And now they are taking away the little that remains of his dignity as a householder and the head of a family, promising him instead Utopias which are called (appropriately enough) "Anticipations" or "News from Nowhere." We come back, in fact, to the main feature which has already been mentioned. The past is communal: the future must be individualist. In the past are all the evils of democracy, variety and violence and doubt, but the future is pure despotism, for the future is pure caprice. Yesterday, I know I was a human fool, but to-morrow I can easily be the Superman.

The modern Englishman, however, is like a man who

should be perpetually kept out, for one reason after another, from the house in which he had meant his married life to begin. This man (Jones let us call him) has always desired the divinely ordinary things; he has married for love, he has chosen or built a small house that fits like a coat; he is ready to be a great grandfather and a local god. And just as he is moving in, something goes wrong. Some tyranny, personal or political, suddenly debars him from the home; and he has to take his meals in the front garden. A passing philosopher (who is also, by a mere coincidence, the man who turned him out) pauses, and leaning elegantly on the railings, explains to him that he is now living that bold life upon the bounty of nature which will be the life of the sublime future. He finds life in the front garden more bold than bountiful, and has to move into mean lodgings in the next street. The philosopher (who turned him out), happening to call at these lodgings, with the probable intention of raising the rent, stops to explain to him that he is now in the real life of mercantile endeavour; the economic struggle between him and the landlady is the only thing out of which, in the sublime future, the wealth of nations can come. He is defeated in the economic struggle, and goes to the workhouse. The philosopher who turned him out (happening at that very moment to be inspecting the workhouse) assures him that he is now at last in that golden republic which is the goal of mankind; he is in an equal, scientific, Socialistic commonwealth, owned by the State and ruled by public officers; in fact, the commonwealth of the sublime future.

Nevertheless, there are signs that the irrational Jones still dreams at night of his old idea of having an ordinary home. He asked for so little, and he has been offered so much. He has been offered bribes of worlds and systems: he has been offered Eden and Utopia and the New Jerusalem, and he only wanted a house; and that has been refused him.

Such an apologue is literally no exaggeration of the facts of English history. The rich did literally turn the poor out of the old guest house on to the road, briefly telling them that it was the road of progress. They did literally force them into factories and the modern wage-slavery, assuring them all the time that this was the only way to wealth and civilisation. Just as they had dragged the rustic from the convent food and ale by saying that the streets of heaven were paved with gold, so now they dragged him from the village food and ale by telling him that the streets of London were paved with gold. As he entered the gloomy porch of Puritanism, so he entered the gloomy porch of Industrialism, being told that each of them was the gate of the future. Hitherto he has only gone from prison to prison, nay, into darkening prisons, for Calvinism opened one small window upon heaven. And now he is asked, in the same educated and authoritative tones, to enter another dark porch, at which he has to surrender into unseen hands his children, his small possessions, and all the habits of his fathers.

Whether this last opening be in truth any more inviting than the old openings of Puritanism and Industrialism can be discussed later. But there can be little doubt, I think, that if some form of Collectivism is imposed upon England it will be imposed, as everything else has been, by an instructed political class upon a people partly apathetic and partly hypnotised. The aristocracy will be as ready to "administer" Collectivism as they were to administer Puritanism or Manchesterism; in some ways such a centralised political power is necessarily attractive to them. It will not be so hard as some innocent Socialists seem to suppose to induce the Honourable Tomnoddy to take over the milk supply as well as the stamp supply—at an increased salary. Mr. Bernard Shaw has remarked that rich men are better than poor men on parish councils because they are free from "financial timidity." Now, the English ruling class is quite free from financial timidity. The Duke of Sussex will be quite ready to be Administrator of Sussex at the same screw. Sir William Harcourt, that typical aristocrat, put it quite correctly. "We" (that is, the aristocracy) "are all Socialists now."

But this is not the essential note on which I desire to end. My main contention is that, whether necessary or not, both Industrialism and Collectivism have been accepted as necessities—not as naked ideals or desires. Nobody liked the Manchester School; it was endured as the only way of producing wealth. Nobody likes the Marxian school; it is endured as the only way of preventing poverty. Nobody's real heart is in the idea of preventing a free man from owning his own farm, or an old woman from cultivating her own garden, any more than anybody's real heart was in the heartless battle of the machines. The purpose of this chapter is sufficiently served in indicating that this proposal also is a *pis aller*, a desperate second best—like teetotalism. I do not propose to prove here that Socialism is a poison; it is enough if I maintain that it is a medicine and not a wine.

The idea of private property universal but private, the idea of families free but still families, of domesticity democratic but still domestic, of one man one house—this remains the real vision and magnet of mankind. The world may accept something more official and general, less human and intimate. But the world will be like a broken-hearted woman who makes a humdrum marriage because she may not make a happy one; Socialism may be the world's deliverance, but it is not the world's desire.

PART II.

IMPERIALISM: OR THE MISTAKE ABOUT MAN

Chapter One

THE CHARM OF JINGOISM

I HAVE cast about widely to find a title for this section; and I confess that the word "Imperialism" is a clumsy version of my meaning. But no other word came nearer; "Militarism" would have been even more misleading, and "The Superman" makes nonsense of any discussion that he enters. Perhaps, upon the whole, the word "Cæsarism" would have been closer; but I desire a popular word; and Imperialism (as the reader will perceive) does cover for the most part the men and theories that I mean to discuss.

This small confusion is increased, however, by the fact that I do also disbelieve in Imperialism, in its popular sense, as a mode or theory of the patriotic sentiment of this country. But popular Imperialism in England has very little to do with the sort of Cæsarean Imperialism I wish to sketch. I differ from the Colonial idealism of Rhodes and Kipling; but I do not think, as some of its opponents do, that it is an insolent creation of English harshness and rapacity. Imperialism, I think, is a fiction created not by English hardness but by English softness; nay, in a sense, by English kindness.

The reasons for believing in Australia are mostly as sentimental as the most sentimental reasons for believing in heaven. New South Wales is quite literally regarded as a place where the wicked cease from troubling and the weary are at rest; that is, a paradise for uncles who have turned dishonest and for nephews who are born tired. British Columbia is in the strict sense a fairy land; it is a world where a magic and irrational luck is supposed to attend the youngest sons. This strange optimism about the ends of the earth is an English weakness; but to show that it is not a coldness or a harshness it is quite sufficient to say that no one shared it more than that gigantic English sentimentalist—the great Charles Dickens. The end of "David Copperfield" is unreal not merely because it is an optimistic ending but because it is an Imperialistic ending. The decorous British happiness planned out for David Copperfield and Agnes would be embarrassed by the perpetual presence of the hopeless tragedy of Emily, or the more hopeless farce of Micawber. Therefore, both Emily and Micawber are shipped off to a vague colony where changes come over them with no conceivable cause, except the climate. The tragic woman becomes contented, and the comic man becomes responsible, solely as the result of a sea voyage and the first sight of a kangaroo.

To Imperialism in the light political sense, therefore, my only objection is that it is an illusion of comfort; that an Empire whose heart is failing should be specially proud of the extremities, is to me no more sublime a fact than that an old dandy whose brain is gone should still be proud of his legs. It consoles men for the evident ugliness and apathy of England with legends of fair youth and heroic strenuousness in distant continents and islands. A man can sit amid the squalor of Seven Dials and feel that life is innocent and godlike in the bush or on the veldt. Just so a man might sit in the squalor of Seven Dials and feel that life was innocent and godlike in Brixton and Surbiton. Brixton and Surbiton are "new"; they are "nearer to nature" in the sense that they have eaten up nature mile by mile. The only objection is the objection of fact. The young men of Brixton are not young giants. The lovers of Surbiton are not all pagan poets, singing with the sweet energy of the spring. Nor are the people of the Colonies when you meet them young giants or pagan poets. They are mostly Cockneys who have lost their last music of real things by getting out of the sound of Bow Bells. Mr. Rudyard Kipling, a man of real though decadent genius, threw a theoretic glamour over them which is already fading. But Mr. Kipling is, in a precise and rather startling sense, the exception that proves the rule. For he has imagination, of an Oriental and cruel kind, but he has it, not because he grew up in a new country but precisely because he grew up in the oldest country upon earth. He is rooted in a past—an Asiatic past. He might never have written "Kabul River" if he had been born in Melbourne.

I say frankly, therefore (lest there should be any air of evasion), that Imperialism in its common patriotic pretensions appears to me both weak and perilous. It is the attempt of a European country to create a kind of sham Europe which it can dominate, instead of the real Europe, which it can only share. It is a love of living with one's inferiors. The notion of restoring the Roman Empire by oneself and for oneself is a dream that has haunted every Christian nation in a different shape and in almost every shape as a snare. The Spanish are a consistent and conservative people; therefore they embodied that attempt at Empire in long and lingering dynasties. The French are a violent people, and therefore they twice conquered that Empire by violence of arms. The English are above all a poetical and optimistic people; and therefore their Empire is something vague and yet sympathetic, something distant and yet dear. But this dream of theirs of being powerful in the uttermost places, though a native weakness, is still a weakness in them; much more of a weakness than gold was to Spain or glory to Napoleon. If ever we were in collision with our real brothers and rivals we should leave all this fancy out of account. We should no more dream of pitting Australian armies against German that of pitting Tasmanian sculpture against French. I have thus explained, lest anyone should accuse me of concealing an unpopular attitude, why I do not believe in Imperialism as commonly understood. I think it not merely an occasional wrong to other peoples but a continuous feebleness, a running sore, in my own. But it is also true that I have dwelt on this Imperialism that is an amiable delusion partly in order to show how different it is from the deeper, more sinister and yet more persuasive thing that I have been forced to call Imperialism for the convenience of this chapter. In order to get to the root of this evil and quite un-English Imperialism we must cast back and begin anew with a more general discussion of the first needs of human intercourse.

Chapter Two

WISDOM AND THE WEATHER

It is admitted, one may hope, that common things are never commonplace. Birth is covered with curtains precisely because it is a staggering and monstrous prodigy. Death and first love, though they happen to everybody, can stop one's heart with the very thought of them. But while this is granted, something further may be claimed. It is not merely true that these universal things are strange; it is, moreover, true that they are subtle. In the last analysis most common things will be found to be highly complicated. Some men of science do indeed get over the difficulty by dealing only with the easy part of it: thus, they will call first love the instinct of sex, and the awe of death the instinct of self-preservation. But this is only getting over the difficulty of describing peacock green by calling it blue. There is blue in it. That there is a strong physical element in both romance and the *Memento Mori* makes them if possible more baffling than if they had been wholly intellectual. No man could say exactly how much his sexuality was coloured by a clean love of beauty, or by the mere boyish itch for irrevocable adventures, like running away to sea. No man could say how far his animal dread of the end was mixed up with

65

mystical traditions touching morals and religion. It is exactly because these things are animal, but not quite animal, that the dance of all the difficulties begins. The materialists analyse the easy part, deny the hard part and go home to their tea.

It is a complete error to suppose that because a thing is vulgar therefore it is not refined; that is, subtle and hard to define. A drawing-room song of my youth which began "In the gloaming, O my darling," was vulgar enough as a song; but the connection between human passion and the twilight is none the less an exquisite and even inscrutable thing. Or to take another obvious instance: the jokes about a mother-in-law are scarcely delicate, but the problem of a mother-in-law is subtle because she is a thing like the twilight. She is a mystical blend of two inconsistent things—law and a mother. The caricatures misrepresent her; but they arise out out of a real human enigma. *Comic Cuts* deals with the difficulty wrongly; but it would need a George Meredith at his best to deal with the difficulty rightly. The nearest statement of the problem perhaps is this: it is not that a mother-in-law must be nasty, but that she must be very nice.

But it is best perhaps to take in illustration some daily custom we have all heard despised as vulgar or trite. Take, for the sake of argument, the custom of talking about the weather. Stevenson calls it "the very nadir and scoff of good conversationalists." Now there are very deep reasons for talking about the weather, reasons that are delicate as well as deep; they lie in layer upon layer of stratified sagacity. First of all it is a gesture of primeval worship. The sky must be invoked; and to begin everything with the weather is a sort of pagan way of beginning everything with prayer. Jones and Brown talk about the weather; but so do Milton and Shelley. Then it is an expression of that elementary idea in politeness—equality. For the very word politeness is only the Greek for citizenship. The word politeness is akin to the word policeman; a charming thought. Properly understood, the citizen should be more polite than the gentleman; perhaps the policeman should be the most courtly and elegant of the three. But all good manners must obviously begin with the sharing of something in a simple style. Two men should share an umbrella; if they have not got an umbrella, they should at least share the rain, with all its rich potentialities of wit and philosophy. "For He maketh His sun to shine . . ." This is the second element in the weather; its recognition of human equality in that we all have our hats under the dark blue spangled umbrella of the universe. Arising out of this is the third wholesome strain in the custom; I mean that it begins with the body and with our inevitable bodily brotherhood. All true friendliness begins with fire and food and drink and the recognition of rain or frost. Those who will not *begin* at the bodily end of things are already prigs and may soon be Christian Scientists. Each human soul has in a sense to enact for itself the gigantic humility of the Incarnation. Every man must descend into the flesh to meet mankind.

Briefly, in the mere observation "a fine day" there is the whole great human idea of comradeship. Now, pure comradeship is another of those broad and yet bewildering things. We all enjoy it; yet when we come to talk about it we almost always talk nonsense, chiefly because we suppose it to be a simpler affair than it is. It is simple to conduct; but it is by no means simple to analyse. Comradeship is at the most only one half of human life; the other half is Love, a thing so different that one might fancy it had been made for another universe. And I do not mean mere sex love; any kind of concentrated passion, maternal love, or even the fiercer kinds of friendship are in their nature alien to pure comradeship. Both sides are essential to life; and both are known in differing degrees to everybody of every age or sex. But very broadly speaking it may still be said that women stand for the dignity of love and men for the dignity of comradeship. I mean that the institution would hardly be respected if the males of the tribe did not mount guard over it. The affections in which women excel have so much more authority and intensity that pure comradeship would be washed away if it were not rallied and guarded in clubs, corps, colleges, banquets and regiments. Most of us have heard the voice in which the hostess tells her husband not to sit too long over the cigars. It is the dreadful voice of Love, seeking to destroy Comradeship.

All true comradeship has in it those three elements which I have remarked in the ordinary exclamation about the weather. First, it has a sort of broad philosophy like the common sky, emphasising that we are all under the same cosmic conditions. We are all in the same boat, the "winged rock" of Mr. Herbert Trench. Secondly, it recognises this bond as the essential one; for comradeship is simply humanity seen in that one aspect in which men are really equal. The old writers were entirely wise when they talked of the equality of men; but they were also very wise in not mentioning women. Women are always authoritarian; they are always above or below; that is why marriage is a sort of poetical see-saw. There are only three things in the world that women do not understand; and they are Liberty, Equality, and Fraternity. But men (a class little understood in the modern world) find these things the breath of their nostrils; and our most learned ladies will not even begin to understand them until they make allowance for this kind of cool camaraderie. Lastly, it contains the third quality of the weather, the insistence upon the body and its indispensable satisfaction. No one has even begun to understand comradeship who does not accept with it a certain hearty eagerness in eating, drinking, or smoking, an uproarious materialism which to many women appears only hoggish. You may call the thing an orgy or a sacrament; it is certainly an essential. It is at root a resistance to the superciliousness of the individual. Nay, its very swaggering and howling are humble. In the heart of its rowdiness there is a sort of mad modesty; a desire to melt the separate soul into the mass of unpretentious masculinity. It is a clamorous confession of the weakness of all flesh. No man must be superior to the things that are common to men. This sort of equality must be bodily and gross and comic. Not only are we all in the same boat, but we are all sea-sick.

The word comradeship just now promises to become as fatuous as the word "affinity." There are clubs of a Socialist sort where all the members, men and women, call each other "Comrade." I have no serious emotions, hostile or otherwise, about this particular habit: at the worst it is conventionality, and at the best flirtation. I am concerned here only to point out a rational principle. If you choose to lump all flowers together, lilies and dahlias and tulips and chrysanthemums and call them all daisies, you will find that you have spoilt the very fine word daisy. If you choose to call every human attachment comradeship, if you include under that name the respect of a youth for a venerable prophetess, the interest of a man in a beautiful woman who bafflles him, the pleasure of a philosophical old fogey in a girl who is impudent and innocent, the end of the meanest quarrel or the beginning of the most mountainous love; if you are going to call all these comradeship, you will gain nothing; you will only lose a word. Daisies are obvious and universal and open; but they are only one kind of flower. Comradeship is obvious and universal and open; but it is only one kind of affection; it has characteristics that would destroy any other kind. Anyone who has known true comradeship in a club or in a regiment, knows that it is impersonal. There is a pedantic phrase used in debating clubs which is strictly true to the masculine emotion; they call it "speaking to the question." Women speak to each other; men speak to the subject they are speaking about. Many an honest man has sat in a ring of his five best friends under heaven and forgotten who was in the room while he explained some system. This is not peculiar to intellectual men; men are all theoretical, whether they are talking about God or about golf. Men are all impersonal; that is to say, republican. No one remembers after a really good talk who has said the good things. Every man speaks to a visionary multitude; a mystical cloud, that is called the club.

It is obvious that this cool and careless quality which is essential to the collective affection of males involves disadvantages and dangers. It leads to spitting; it leads to coarse speech; it must lead to these things so long as it is honourable; comradeship must be in some degree ugly. The moment beauty is mentioned in male friendship, the nostrils are stopped with the smell of abominable things. Friendship must be physically dirty if it is to be morally clean. It must be in its shirt sleeves. The chaos of habits that always goes with males when left entirely to themselves has only one honourable cure; and that is the strict discipline of a monastery. Anyone who has seen our unhappy young idealists in East End Settlements losing their collars in the wash and living on tinned salmon, will fully understand why it was decided by the wisdom of St. Bernard or St. Benedict, that if men were to live without women, they must not live without rules. Something of the same sort of artificial exactitude, of course, is obtained in an army; and an army also has to be in many ways monastic; only that it has celibacy without chastity. But these things do not apply to normal or married men. These have quite sufficient restraint on their instinctive anarchy in the savage common sense of the other sex. There is only one very timid sort of man that is not afraid of women.

Chapter Three

THE COMMON VISION

Now this masculine love of an open and level camaraderie is the life within all democracies and attempts to govern by debate; without it the republic would be a dead formula. Even as it is, of course, the spirit of democracy frequently differs widely from the letter, and a pothouse is often a better test than a Parliament. Democracy in its human sense is not arbitrament by the majority; it is not even arbitrament by everybody. It can be more nearly defined as arbitrament by anybody. I mean that it rests on that club habit of taking a total stranger for granted, of assuming certain things to be inevitably common to yourself and him. Only the things that anybody may be presumed to hold have the full authority of democracy. Look out of the window and notice the first man who walks by. The Liberals may have swept England with an overwhelming majority; but you would not stake a button that the man is a Liberal. The Bible may be read in all schools and respected in all law courts; but you would not bet a straw that he believes in the Bible. But you would bet your week's wages, let us say, that he believes in wearing clothes. You would bet that he believes that physical courage is a fine thing, or that parents have authority over children. Of course, he might be the millionth man who does not believe these things; if it comes to that, he might be the Bearded Lady dressed up as a man. But these prodigies are quite a different thing from any mere calculation of numbers. People who hold these views are not a minority, but a monstrosity. But of these universal dogmas that have full democratic authority the only test is this test of anybody. What you would observe before any new-comer in a tavern —that is the real English law. The first man you see from the window, he is the King of England.

The decay of taverns, which is but a part of the general decay of democracy, has undoubtedly weakened this masculine spirit of equality. I remember that a roomful of Socialists literally laughed when I told them that there were no two nobler words in all poetry than Public House. They thought it was a joke. Why *they* should think it a joke, since they want to make all houses public houses, I cannot imagine. But if anyone wishes to see the real rowdy egalitarianism which is necessary (to males, at least) he can find it as well as anywhere in the great old tavern disputes which come down to us in such books as Boswell's Johnson. It is worth while to mention that one name especially, because the modern world in its morbidity has done it a strange injustice. The demeanour of Johnson, it is said, was "harsh and despotic." It was occasionally harsh, but it was never despotic. Johnson was not in the least a despot; Johnson was a demagogue, he shouted against a shouting crowd. The very fact that he wrangled with other people is proof that other people were allowed to wrangle with him. His very brutality was based on the idea of an equal scrimmage, like that of football. It is strictly true that he bawled and banged the table because he was a modest man. He was honestly afraid of being overwhelmed or even overlooked. Addison had exquisite manners and was the king of his company. He was polite to everybody, but superior to everybody; therefore he has been handed down for ever in the immortal insult of Pope—

> "Like Cato, give his little senate laws,
> And sit attentive to his own applause."

Johnson, so far from being king of his company, was a sort of Irish Member in his own Parliament. Addison was a courteous superior and was hated. Johnson was an insolent equal, and therefore was loved by all who knew him and handed down in a marvellous book which is one of the mere miracles of love.

This doctrine of equality is essential to conversation; so much may be admitted by anyone who knows what conversation is. Once arguing at a table in a tavern, the most famous man on earth would wish to be obscure, so that his brilliant remarks might blaze like stars on the background of his obscurity. To anything worth calling a man nothing can be conceived more cold or cheerless than to be king of your company. But it may be said that in masculine sports and games, other than the great game of debate, there is definite emulation and eclipse. There is indeed emulation, but this is only an ardent sort of equality. Games are competitive, because that is the only way of making them exciting. But if anyone doubts that men must for ever return to the ideal of equality, it is only necessary to answer that there is such a thing as a handicap. If men exulted in mere superiority, they would seek to see how far such superiority could go; they would be glad when one strong runner came in miles ahead of all the rest. But what men like is not the triumph of superiors, but the struggle of equals; and, therefore, they introduce even into their competitive sports an artificial equality.

It is sad to think how few of those who arrange our sporting handicaps can be supposed with any probability to realise that they are abstract, and even severe, republicans.

No; the real objection to equality and selfrule has nothing to do with any of these free and festive aspects of mankind; all men are democrats when they are happy. The philosophic opponent of democracy would substantially sum up his position by saying that it "will not work." Before going further, I will register in passing a protest against the assumption that working is the one test of humanity. Heaven does not work; it plays. Men are most themselves when they are free; and if I find that men are snobs in their work but democrats on their holidays, I shall take the liberty to believe their holidays. But it is this question of work which really perplexes the question of equality; and it is with that that we must now deal. Perhaps the truth can be put most pointedly thus: that democracy has one real enemy, and that is civilisation. Those utilitarian miracles which science has made are anti-democratic, not so much in their perversion, or even in their practical result, as in their primary shape and purpose. The Frame-Breaking Rioters were right; not perhaps in thinking that machines would make fewer men workmen; but certainly in thinking that machines would make fewer men masters. More wheels do mean fewer handles; fewer handles do mean fewer hands. The machinery of science must be individualistic and isolated. A mob can shout round a palace; but a mob cannot shout down a telephone. The specialist appears, and democracy is half spoilt at a stroke.

Chapter Four

THE INSANE NECESSITY

THE common conception among the dregs of Darwinian culture is that men have slowly worked their way out of inequality into a state of comparative equality. The truth is, I fancy, almost exactly the opposite. All men have normally and naturally begun with the idea of equality; they have only abandoned it late and reluctantly, and always for some material reason of detail. They have never naturally felt that one class of men was superior to another; they have always been driven to assume it through certain practical limitations of space and time.

For example, there is one element which must always tend to oligarchy—or rather to despotism; I mean the element of hurry. If the house has caught fire a man must ring up the fire engines; a committee cannot ring them up. If a camp is surprised by night somebody must give the order to fire; there is no time to vote it. It is solely a question of the physical limitations of time and space; not at all of any mental limitations in the mass of men commanded. If all the people in the house were men of destiny it would still be better that they should not all talk into the telephone at once; nay, it would be better that the silliest man of all should speak uninterrupted. If an army actually consisted of nothing but Hannibals and Napoleons, it would still be better in the case of a surprise that they should not all give orders together. Nay, it would be better if the stupidest of them all give the orders. Thus, we see that merely military subordination, so far from resting on the inequality of men, actually rests on the equality of men. Discipline does not involve the Carlylean notion that somebody is always right when everybody is wrong, and that we must discover and crown that somebody. On the contrary, discipline means that in certain frightfully rapid circumstances, one can trust anybody so long as he is not everybody. The military spirit does not mean (as Carlyle fancied) obeying the strongest and wisest man. On the contrary, the military spirit means, if anything, obeying the weakest and stupidest man, obeying him merely because he is a man, and not a thousand men. Submission to a weak man is discipline. Submission to a strong man is only servility.

Now it can be easily shown that the thing we call aristocracy in Europe is not in its origin and spirit an aristocracy at all. It is not a system of spiritual degrees and distinctions like, for example, the caste system of India, or even like the old Greek distinction between free-men and slaves. It is simply the remains of a military organisation, framed partly to sustain the sinking Roman Empire, partly to break and avenge the awful onslaught of Islam. The word Duke simply means Colonel, just as the word Emperor simply means Commander-in-Chief. The whole story is told in the single title of Counts of the Holy Roman Empire, which merely means officers in the European army against the contemporary Yellow Peril. Now in an army nobody ever dreams of supposing that difference of rank represents a difference of moral reality. Nobody ever says about a regiment, "Your

Major is very humorous and energetic; your Colonel, of course, must be even more humorous and yet more energetic." No one ever says, in reporting a mess-room conversation, "Lieutenant Jones was very witty, but was naturally inferior to Captain Smith." The essence of an army is the idea of official inequality, founded on unofficial equality. The Colonel is not obeyed because he is the best man, but because he is the Colonel. Such was probably the spirit of the system of dukes and counts when it first arose out of the military spirit and military necessities of Rome. With the decline of those necessities it has gradually ceased to have meaning as a military organisation, and become honeycombed with unclean plutocracy. Even now it is not a spiritual aristocracy—it is not so bad as all that. It is simply an army without an enemy—billeted upon the people.

Man, therefore, has a specialist as well as comrade-like aspect; and the case of militarism is not the only case of such specialist submission. The tinker and tailor, as well as the soldier and sailor, require a certain rigidity of rapidity of action: at least, if the tinker is not organised that is largely why he does not tink on any large scale. The tinker and tailor often represent the two nomadic races in Europe: the Gipsy and the Jew; but the Jew alone has influence because he alone accepts some sort of discipline. Man, we say, has two sides, the specialist side where he must have subordination, and the social side where he must have equality. There is a truth in the saying that nine tailors go to make a man; but we must remember also that nine Poets Laureate or nine Astronomers Royal go to make a man too. Nine million tradesmen go to make Man himself; but humanity consists of tradesmen when they are not talking shop. Now the peculiar peril of our time, which I call for argument's sake Im-

perialism or Cæsarism, is the complete eclipse of comradeship and equality by specialism and domination.

There are only two kinds of social structure conceivable
—personal government and impersonal government. If my
anarchic friends will not have rules—they will have rulers.
Preferring personal government, with its tact and flexibility,
is called Royalism. Preferring impersonal government, with
its dogmas and definitions, is called Republicanism. Object-
ing broadmindedly both to kings and creeds is called Bosh;
at least, I know no more philosophic word for it. You can be
guided by the shrewdness or presence of mind of one ruler,
or by the equality and ascertained justice of one rule; but
you must have one or the other, or you are not a nation, but
a nasty mess. Now men in their aspect of equality and debate adore the idea of rules; they develop and complicate
them greatly to excess. A man finds far more regulations and
definitions in his club, where there are rules, than in his
home, where there is a ruler. A deliberative assembly, the
House of Commons, for instance, carries this mummery to
the point of a methodical madness. The whole system is stiff
with rigid unreason; like the Royal Court in Lewis Carroll.
You would think the Speaker would speak; therefore he is
mostly silent. You would think a man would take off his hat
to stop and put it on to go away; therefore he takes off his
hat to walk out and puts it on to stop in. Names are forbidden, and a man must call his own father "my right honourable friend the member for West Birmingham." These are,
perhaps, fantasies of decay: but fundamentally they answer
a masculine appetite. Men feel that rules, even if irrational,
are universal; men feel that law is equal, even when it is not
equitable. There is a wild fairness in the thing—as there is
in tossing up.

Again, it is gravely unfortunate that when critics do attack

such cases as the Commons it is always on the points (perhaps the few points) where the Commons are right. They
denounce the House as the Talking-Shop, and complain that
it wastes time in wordy mazes. Now this is just one respect
in which the Commons are actually like the Common People. If they love leisure and long debate, it is because all
men love it; there they really represent England. There
the Parliament does approach to the virile virtues of the
pothouse.

The real truth is that adumbrated in the introductory section, when we spoke of the sense of home and property, as
now we speak of the sense of counsel and community. All
men do naturally love the idea of leisure, laughter, loud and
equal argument; but there stands a spectre in our hall: we
are conscious of the towering modern challenge that is
called specialism or cut-throat competition—Business. Business will have nothing to do with leisure; business will have
no truck with comradeship; business will pretend to no patience with all the legal fictions and fantastic handicaps by
which comradeship protects its egalitarian ideal. The modern millionaire, when engaged in the agreeable and typical
task of sacking his own father, will certainly not refer to him
as the right honourable clerk from the Laburnum Road,
Brixton. Therefore there has arisen in modern life a literary
fashion devoting itself to the romance of business, to great
demigods of greed and to the fairyland of finance. This
popular philosophy is utterly despotist and anti-democratic;
this fashion is the flower of that Cæsarism against which I
am concerned to protest. The ideal millionaire is strong in
the possession of a brain of steel. The fact that the real millionaire is rather more often strong in the possession of a
head of wood, does not alter the spirit and trend of the
idolatry. The essential argument is "Specialists must be

despots; men must be specialists. You cannot have equality
in a soap factory; so you cannot have it anywhere. You cannot have comradeship in a wheat corner; so you cannot have
it at all. We must have commerical civilisation; therefore we
must destroy democracy." I know that plutocrats have seldom sufficient fancy to soar to such examples as soap or
wheat. They generally confine themselves, with fine fresh-
ness of mind, to a comparison between the state and a ship.
One anti-democratic writer remarked that he would not
like to sail in a vessel in which the cabin-boy had an equal
vote with the captain. It might easily be urged in answer
that many a ship (the *Victoria*, for instance) was sunk because an admiral gave an order which a cabin-boy could see
was wrong. But this is a debating reply; the essential fallacy
is both deeper and simpler. The elementary fact is that we
were all born in a state; we were not all born on a ship, like
some of our great British bankers. A ship still remains a
specialist experiment, like a diving-bell or a flying ship: in
such peculiar perils the need for promptitude constitutes the
need for autocracy. But we live and die in the vessel of the
state; and if we cannot find freedom, camaraderie and the
popular element in the state, we cannot find it at all. And
the modern doctrine of commercial despotism means that
we shall not find it at all. Our specialist trades in their
highly civilised state cannot (it says) be run without the
whole brutal business of bossing and sacking, "too old at
forty" and all the rest of the filth. And they must be run,
and therefore we call on Cæsar. Nobody but the Superman
could descend to do such dirty work.

Now (to reiterate my title) this is what is wrong. This is
the huge modern heresy of altering the human soul to fit its
conditions, instead of altering human conditions to fit the
human soul. If soap-boiling is really inconsistent with

brotherhood, so much the worse for soap-boiling, not for brotherhood. If civilisation really cannot get on with democracy, so much the worse for civilisation, not for democracy. Certainly, it would be far better to go back to village communes, if they really are communes. Certainly, it would be better to do without soap rather than to do without society. Certainly, we would sacrifice all our wires, wheels, systems, specialities, physical science and frenzied finance for one half-hour of happiness such as has often come to us with comrades in a common tavern. I do not say the sacrifice will be necessary; I only say it will be easy.

PART III.

FEMINISM: OR THE MISTAKE ABOUT WOMAN

Chapter One

THE UNMILITARY SUFFRAGETTE

IT will be better to adopt in this chapter the same process that appeared a piece of mental justice in the last. My general opinions on the feminine question are such as many Suffragists would warmly approve; and it would be easy to state them without any open reference to the current controversy. But just as it seemed more decent to say first that I was not in favour of Imperialism even in its practical and popular sense, so it seems more decent to say the same of Female Suffrage, in its practical and popular sense. In other words, it is only fair to state, however hurriedly, the superficial objection to the "Suffragettes" before we go on to the really subtle questions behind the Suffrage.

Well, to get this honest but unpleasant business over, the objection to the Suffragettes is not that they are Militant Suffragettes. On the contrary, it is that they are not militant enough. A revolution is a military thing; it has all the military virtues; one of which is that it comes to an end. Two parties fight with deadly weapons; but under certain rules of arbitrary honour, the party that wins becomes the government and proceeds to govern. The aim of civil war, like the aim of all war, is peace. Now the Suffragettes cannot raise civil war in this soldierly and decisive sense; first, because they are women; and, secondly, because they are very few women. But they can raise something else; which is altogether another pair of shoes. They do not create revolution; what they do create is anarchy; and the difference between these is not a question of violence, but a question of fruitfulness and finality. Revolution of its nature produces government; anarchy only produces more anarchy. Men may have what opinions they please about the beheading of King Charles or King Louis, but they cannot deny that Bradshaw and Cromwell ruled, that Carnot and Napoleon governed. Someone conquered; something occurred. You can only knock off the King's head once. But you can knock off the King's hat any number of times. Destruction is finite; obstruction is infinite: so long as rebellion takes the form of mere disorder (instead of an attempt to enforce a new order) there is no logical end to it; it can feed on itself and renew itself for ever. If Napoleon had not wanted to be a Consul, but only wanted to be a nuisance, he could, possibly, have prevented any government arising successfully out of the Revolution. But such a proceeding would not have deserved the dignified name of rebellion.

It is exactly this unmilitant quality in the Suffragettes that makes their superficial problem. The problem is that their action has none of the advantages of ultimate violence; it does not afford a test. War is a dreadful thing; but it does prove two points sharply and unanswerably—numbers, and an unnatural valour. One does discover the two urgent matters; how many rebels there are alive, and how many are ready to be dead. But a tiny minority, even an interested minority, may maintain mere disorder for ever. There is also, of course, in the case of these women, the further falsity that is introduced by their sex. It is false to state the matter as a mere brutal question of strength. If his muscles give a man a vote, then his horse ought to have two votes and his elephant five votes. The truth is more subtle than that; it is that bodily outbreak is a man's instinctive weapon, like the hoofs to the horse or the tusks to the elephant. All riot is a threat of war; but the woman is brandishing a weapon she can never use. There are many weapons that she could and does use. If (for example) all the women nagged for a vote they would get it in a month. But there again, one must remember, it would be necessary to get all the women to nag. And that brings us to the end of the political surface of the matter. The working objection to the Suffragette philosophy is simply that over-mastering millions of women do not agree with it. I am aware that some maintain that women ought to have votes whether the majority wants them or not; but this is surely a strange and childish case of setting up formal democracy to the destruction of actual democracy. What should the mass of women decide if they do not decide their general place in the State? These people practically say that females may vote about everything except about Female Suffrage.

But having again cleared my conscience of my merely political and possibly unpopular opinion, I will again cast back and try to treat the matter in a slower and more sympathetic style; attempt to trace the real roots of woman's position in the Western state, and the causes of our existing traditions or perhaps prejudices upon the point. And for this purpose it is again necessary to travel far from the modern topic, the mere Suffragette of to-day, and to go back to subjects which, though much more old, are, I think, considerably more fresh.

Chapter Two

THE UNIVERSAL STICK

CAST your eye round the room in which you sit, and select some three or four things that have been with man almost since his beginning; which at least we hear of early in the centuries and often among the tribes. Let me suppose that you see a knife on the table, a stick in the corner, or a fire on the hearth. About each of these you will notice one speciality; that not one of them is special. Each of these ancestral things is a universal thing; made to supply many different needs; and while tottering pedants nose about to find the cause and origin of some old custom, the truth is that it had fifty causes or a hundred origins. The knife is meant to cut wood, to cut cheese, to cut pencils, to cut throats; for a myriad ingenious or innocent human objects. The stick is meant partly to hold a man up, partly to knock a man down; partly to point with like a finger-post, partly to balance with like a balancing pole, partly to trifle with like a cigarette, partly to kill with like the club of a giant; it is a crutch and a cudgel; an elongated finger and an extra leg. The case is the same, of course, with the fire, about which the strangest modern views have arisen. A queer fancy seems to be current that a fire exists to warm people. It exists to warm people, to light their darkness, to raise their spirits, to toast their muffins, to air their rooms, to cook their chestnuts, to tell stories to their children, to make chequered shadows on their walls, to boil their hurried kettles, and to be the red heart of a man's house and that hearth for which, as the great heathens said, a man should die.

Now it is the great mark of our modernity that people are always proposing substitutes for these old things; and these substitutes always answer one purpose where the old thing answered ten. The modern man will wave a cigarette instead of a stick; he will cut his pencil with a little screwing pencil-sharpener instead of a knife; and he will even boldly offer to be warmed by hot water pipes instead of a fire. I have my doubts about pencil-sharpeners even for sharpening pencils; and about hot water pipes even for heat. But when we think of all those other requirements that these institutions answered, there opens before us the whole horrible harlequinade of our civilisation. We see as in a vision a world where a man tries to cut his throat with a pencil-sharpener; where a man must learn single-stick with a cigarette; where a man must try to toast muffins at electric lamps, and see red and golden castles in the surface of hot water pipes.

The principle of which I speak can be seen everywhere in a comparison between the ancient and universal things and the modern and specialist things. The object of a theodolite is to lie level; the object of a stick is to swing loose at any angle; to whirl like the very wheel of liberty. The object of a lancet is to lance; when used for slashing, gashing, ripping, lopping off heads and limbs, it is a disappointing instrument. The object of an electric light is merely to light (a despicable modesty); and the object of an asbestos stove. . . . I wonder what is the object of an asbestos stove? If a man found a coil of rope in a desert he could at least think of all the things that can be done with a coil of rope; and some of them might even be practical. He could tow a boat or lasso a horse. He could play cat's-cradle, or pick oakum. He could construct a rope-ladder for an eloping heiress, or cord her boxes for a travelling maiden aunt. He could learn to tie a bow, or he could hang himself. Far otherwise with the unfortunate traveller who should find a telephone in the desert. You can telephone with a telephone; you cannot do anything else with it. And though this is one of the wildest joys of life, it falls by one degree from its full delirium when there is nobody to answer you. The contention is, in brief, that you must pull up a hundred roots, and not one, before you uproot any of these hoary and simple expedients. It is only with great difficulty that a modern scientific sociologist can be got to see that any old method has a leg to stand on. But almost every old method has four or five legs to stand on. Almost all the old institutions are quadrupeds; and some of them are centipedes.

Consider these cases, old and new, and you will observe the operation of a general tendency. Everywhere there was one big thing that served six purposes; everywhere now there are six small things; or, rather (and there is the trouble), there are just five and a half. Nevertheless, we will not say that this separation and specialism is entirely useless or inexcusable. I have often thanked God for the telephone; I may any day thank God for the lancet; and there is none of these brilliant and narrow inventions (except, of course, the asbestos stove) which might not be at some moment necessary and lovely. But I do not think the most austere upholder of specialism will deny that there is in these old, many-sided institutions an element of unity and universality which may well be preserved in its due proportion and place. Spiritually, at least, it will be admitted that some all-round balance is needed to equalise the extravagance of experts. It would not be difficult to carry the parable of the knife and stick into higher regions. Religion, the immortal maiden, has been a maid-of-all-work as well as a servant of mankind. She provided men at once with the theoretic laws of an unalterable cosmos; and also with the practical rules of the rapid and thrilling game of morality. She taught logic to the student and told fairy tales to the children; it was her business to confront the nameless gods whose fear is on all flesh, and also to see the streets were spotted with silver and scarlet, that there was a day for wearing ribbons or an hour for ringing bells. The large uses of religion have been broken up into lesser specialities, just as the uses of the hearth have been broken up into hot water pipes and electric bulbs. The romance of ritual and coloured emblem has been taken over by that narrowest of all trades, modern art (the sort called art for art's sake), and men are in modern practice informed that they may use all symbols, so long as they mean nothing by them. The romance of conscience has been dried up into the science of ethics; which may well be called decency for decency's sake, decency unborn of cosmic energies and barren of artistic flower. The cry to the dim gods, cut off from ethics and cosmology, has become mere Psychical Research. Everything has been sundered from everything else, and everything has grown cold. Soon we shall hear of specialists dividing the tune from the words of a song, on the ground that they spoil each other; and I did once meet a man who openly advocated the separation of almonds and raisins. This world is all one wild divorce court; nevertheless, there are many who still hear in their souls the thunder of the authority of human habit; those whom Man hath joined let no man sunder.

This book must avoid religion, but there must (I say) be many, religious and irreligious, who will concede that this power of answering many purposes was a sort of strength which should not wholly die out of our lives. As a part of personal character, even the moderns will agree that many-sidedness is a merit and a merit that may easily be overlooked. This balance and universality has been the vision of many groups of men in many ages. It was the Liberal Education of Aristotle; the jack-of-all-trades artistry of Leonardo da Vinci and his friends; the august amateurishness of the Cavalier Person of Quality like Sir William Temple or the great Earl of Dorset. It has appeared in literature in our time in the most erratic and opposite shapes, set to almost inaudible music by Walter Pater and enunciated through a fog-horn by Walt Whitman. But the great mass of men have always been unable to achieve this literal universality, because of the nature of their work in the world. Not, let it be noted, because of the existence of their work. Leonardo da Vinci must have worked pretty hard; on the other hand many a government office clerk, village constable or elusive plumber may do (to all human appearance) no work at all, and yet show no signs of the Aristotelian universalism. What makes it difficult for the average man to be a universalist is that the average man has to be a specialist; he has not only to learn one trade but to learn it so well as to uphold him in a more or less ruthless society. This is generally true of males from the first hunter to the last electrical engineer; each has not merely to act, but to excel. Nimrod has not only to be a mighty hunter before the Lord, but also a mighty hunter before the other hunters. The electrical engineer has to be a very electrical engineer or he is outstripped by engineers yet more electrical. Those very miracles of the human mind on which the modern world prides itself, and rightly in the main, would be impossible without a certain concentration which disturbs the pure balance of reason more than does religious bigotry. No creed can be so limiting as that awful adjuration that the cobbler must not go beyond his last. So the largest and wildest shots of our world are but in one direction and with a defined trajectory: the gunner cannot go beyond his shot, and his shot so often falls short; the astronomer cannot go beyond his telescope, and his telescope goes such a little way. All these are like men who have stood on the high peak of a mountain and seen the horizon like a single ring and who then descend down different paths towards different towns, travelling slow or fast. It is right; there must be people travelling to different towns; there must be specialists; but shall no one behold the horizon? Shall all mankind be specialist surgeons or peculiar plumbers; shall all humanity be monomaniac? Tradition has decided that only half of humanity shall be monomaniac. It has decided that in every home there shall be a tradesman and a Jack-of-all-trades. But it has also decided, among other things, that the Jack-of-all-trades shall be a Jill-of-all-trades. It has decided, rightly or wrongly, that this specialism and this universalism shall be divided between the sexes. Cleverness shall be left for men and wisdom for women. For cleverness kills wisdom; that is one of the few sad and certain things.

But for women this ideal of comprehensive capacity (or common sense) must long ago have been washed away. It must have melted in the frightful furnaces of ambition and eager technicality. A man must be partly a one-idead man, because he is a one-weaponed man—and he is flung naked into the fight. The world's demand comes to him direct; to his wife indirectly. In short, he must (as the books on Success say) give "his best"; and what a small part of a man

"his best" is! His second and third best are often much better. If he is the first violin he must fiddle for life; he must
not remember that he is a fine fourth bag-pipe, a fair fif-
teenth billiard-cue, a foil, a fountain-pen, a hand at whist, a
gun, and an image of God.

Chapter Three

THE EMANCIPATION OF DOMESTICITY

AND it should be remarked in passing that this force upon a man to develop one feature has nothing to do with what is commonly called our competitive system, but would equally exist under any rationally conceivable kind of Collectivism. Unless the Socialists are frankly ready for a fall in the standard of violins, telescopes and electric lights, they must somehow create a moral demand on the individual that he shall keep up his present concentration on these things. It was only by men being in some degree specialist that there ever were any telescopes; they must certainly be in some degree specialist in order to keep them going. It is not by making a man a State wage-earner that you can prevent him thinking principally about the very difficult way he earns his wages. There is only one way to preserve in the world that high levity and that more leisurely outlook which fulfils the old vision of universalism. That is, to permit the existence of a partly protected half of humanity; a half which the harassing industrial demand troubles indeed, but only troubles indirectly. In other words, there must be in every centre of humanity one human being upon a larger plan; one who does not "give her best," but gives her all.

Our old analogy of the fire remains the most workable one. The fire need not blaze like electricity nor boil like boiling water; its point is that it blazes more than water and warms more than light. The wife is like the fire, or to put things in their proper proportion, the fire is like the wife. Like the fire, the woman is expected to cook: not to excel in cooking, but to cook; to cook better than her husband who is earning the coke by lecturing on botany or breaking stones. Like the fire, the woman is expected to tell tales to the children, not original and artistic tales, but tales—better tales than would probably be told by a first-class cook. Like the fire, the woman is expected to illuminate and ventilate, not by the most startling revelations or the wildest winds of thought, but better than a man can do it after breaking stones or lecturing. But she cannot be expected to endure anything like this universal duty if she is also to endure the direct cruelty of competitive or bureaucratic toil. Woman must be a cook, but not a competitive cook; a school-mistress, but not a competitive school-mistress; a house-decorator, but not a competitive house-decorator; a dressmaker, but not a competitive dressmaker. She should have not one trade but twenty hobbies; she, unlike the man, may develop all her second bests. This is what has been really aimed at from the first in what is called the seclusion, or even the oppression, of women. Women were not kept at home in order to keep them narrow; on the contrary, they were kept at home in order to keep them broad. The world outside the home was one mass of narrowness, a maze of cramped paths, a madhouse of monomaniacs. It was only by partly limiting and protecting the woman that she was enabled to play at five or six professions and so come almost as near to God as the child when he plays at a hundred trades. But the woman's professions, unlike the child's, were all truly and almost terribly fruitful; so tragically real that nothing but her universality and balance prevented them being merely morbid.

This is the substance of the contention I offer about the historic female position. I do not deny that women have been wronged and even tortured; but I doubt if they were ever tortured so much as they are tortured now by the absurd modern attempt to make them domestic empresses and competitive clerks at the same time. I do not deny that even under the old tradition women had a harder time than men; that is why we take off our hats. I do not deny that all these various female functions were exasperating; but I say that there was some aim and meaning in keeping them various. I do not pause even to deny that woman was a servant; but at least she was a general servant.

The shortest way of summarising the position is to say that woman stands for the idea of Sanity; that intellectual home to which the mind must return after every excursion on extravagance. The mind that finds its way to wild places is the poet's; but the mind that never finds its way back is the lunatic's. There must in every machine be a part that moves and a part that stands still; there must be in everything that changes a part that is unchangeable. And many of the phenomena which moderns hastily condemn are really parts of this position of the woman as the centre and pillar of health. Much of what is called her subservience, and even her pliability, is merely the subservience and pliability of a universal remedy; she varies as medicines vary, with the disease. She has to be an optimist to the morbid husband, a salutary pessimist to the happy-go-lucky husband. She has to prevent the Quixote from being put upon, and the bully from putting upon others. The French King wrote—

"Toujours femme varie
Bien fol qui s'y fie,"

but the truth is that woman always varies, and that is exactly why we always trust her. To correct every adventure and extravagance with its antidote in common sense is not (as the moderns seem to think) to be in the position of a spy or a slave. It is to be in the position of Aristotle or (at the lowest) Herbert Spencer, to be a universal morality, a complete system of thought. The slave flatters; the complete moralist rebukes. It is, in short, to be a Trimmer in the true sense of that honourable term; which for some reason or other is always used in a sense exactly opposite to its own. It seems really to be supposed that a Trimmer means a cowardly person who always goes over to the stronger side. It really means a highly chivalrous person who always goes over to the weaker side; like one who trims a boat by sitting where there are few people seated. Woman is a Trimmer; and it is a generous, dangerous and romantic trade.

The final fact which fixes this is a sufficiently plain one. Supposing it to be conceded that humanity has acted at least not unnaturally in dividing itself into two halves, respectively typifying the ideals of special talent and of general sanity (since they are genuinely difficult to combine completely in one mind), it is not difficult to see why the line of cleavage has followed the line of sex, or why the female became the emblem of the universal and the male of the special and superior. Two gigantic facts of nature fixed it thus: first, that the woman who frequently fulfilled her functions literally *could* not be specially prominent in experiment and adventure; and second, that the same natural operation surrounded her with very young children, who require to be taught not so much anything as everything.

Babies need not to be taught a trade, but to be introduced to a world. To put the matter shortly, woman is generally shut up in a house with a human being at the time when he asks all the questions that there are, and some that there aren't. It would be odd if she retained any of the narrowness of a specialist. Now if anyone says that this duty of general enlightenment (even when freed from modern rules and hours, and exercised more spontaneously by a more protected person) is in itself too exacting and oppressive, I can understand the view. I can only answer that our race has thought it worth while to cast this burden on women in order to keep common sense in the world. But when people begin to talk about this domestic duty as not merely difficult but trivial and dreary, I simply give up the question. For I cannot with the utmost energy of imagination conceive what they mean. When domesticity, for instance, is called drudgery, all the difficulty arises from a double meaning in the word. If drudgery only means dreadfully hard work, I admit the woman drudges in the home, as a man might drudge at the Cathedral of Amiens or drudge behind a gun at Trafalgar. But if it means that the hard work is more heavy because it is trifling, colourless and of small import to the soul, then, as I say, I give it up; I do not know what the words mean. To be Queen Elizabeth within a definite area, deciding sales, banquets, labours and holidays; to be Whiteley within a certain area, providing toys, boots, sheets, cakes and books; to be Aristotle within a certain area, teaching morals, manners, theology, and hygiene; I can understand how this might exhaust the mind, but I cannot imagine how it could narrow it. How can it be a large career to tell other people's children about the Rule of Three, and a small career to tell one's own children about the universe? How can it be broad to be the same thing to everyone, and narrow to be everything to someone? No; a woman's function is laborious, but because it is gigantic, not because it is minute. I will pity Mrs. Jones for the hugeness of her task; I will never pity her for its smallness.

But though the essential of the woman's task is universality, this does not, of course, prevent her from having one or two severe though largely wholesome prejudices. She has, on the whole, been more conscious than man that she is only one half of humanity; but she has expressed it (if one may say so of a lady) by getting her teeth into the two or three things which she thinks she stands for. I would observe here in parentheses that much of the recent official trouble about women has arisen from the fact that they transfer to things of doubt and reason that sacred stubbornness only proper to the primary things which a woman was set to guard. One's own children, one's own altar, ought to be a matter of principle—or, if you like, a matter of prejudice. On the other hand, who wrote Junius's Letters ought not to be a principle or a prejudice, it ought to be a matter of free and almost indifferent inquiry. But make an energetic modern girl secretary to a league to show that George III. wrote Junius, and in three months she will believe it too, out of mere loyalty to her employers. Modern women defend their office with all the fierceness of domesticity. They fight for desk and typewriter as for hearth and home, and develop a sort of wolfish wifehood on behalf of the invisible head of the firm. That is why they do office work so well; and that is why they ought not to do it.

Chapter Four

THE ROMANCE OF THRIFT

THE larger part of womankind, however, have had to fight
for things slightly more intoxicating to the eye than the desk
or the typewriter; and it cannot be denied that in defending
these, women have developed the quality called prejudice
to a powerful and even menacing degree. But these prejudices will always be found to fortify the main position of
the woman, that she is to remain a general overseer, an
autocrat within small compass but on all sides. On the one
or two points on which she really misunderstands the man's
position, it is almost entirely in order to preserve her own.
The two points on which woman, actually and of herself, is
most tenacious may be roughly summarised as the ideal of
thrift and the ideal of dignity.

Unfortunately for this book it is written by a male, and
these two qualities, if not hateful to a man, are at least hateful in a man. But if we are to settle the sex question at all
fairly, all males must make an imaginative attempt to enter
into the attitude of all good women towards these two things.
The difficulty exists especially, perhaps, in the thing called
thrift; we men have so much encouraged each other in
throwing money right and left, that there has come at last

to be a sort of chivalrous and poetical air about losing six-
pence. But on a broader and more candid consideration the
case scarcely stands so.

Thrift is the really romantic thing; economy is more romantic than extravagance. Heaven knows I for one speak
disinterestedly in the matter; for I cannot clearly remember
saving a half-penny ever since I was born. But the thing is
true; economy, properly understood, is the more poetic.
Thrift is poetic because it is creative; waste is unpoetic because it is waste. It is prosaic to throw money away because
it is prosaic to throw anything away; it is negative; it is a confession of indifference, that is, it is a confession of failure.
The most prosaic thing about the house is the dustbin, and
the one great objection to the new fastidious and æsthetic
homestead is simply that in such a moral *ménage* the dustbin
must be bigger than the house. If a man could undertake to
make use of all the things in his dustbin he would be a
broader genius than Shakespeare. When science began to
use by-products; when science found that colours could be
made out of coal-tar, she made her greatest and perhaps her
only claim on the real respect of the human soul. Now the
aim of the good woman is to use the by-products, or, in other
words, to rummage in the dustbin.

A man can only fully comprehend it if he thinks of some
sudden joke or expedient got up with such materials as may
be found in a private house on a rainy day. A man's definite
daily work is generally run with such rigid conveniences of
modern science that thrift, the picking up of potential helps
here and there, has almost become unmeaning to him. He
comes across it most (as I say) when he is playing some
game within four walls; when in charades, a hearthrug will
just do for a fur coat, or a tea-cosy just do for a cocked hat;
when a toy theatre needs timber and cardboard, and the

house has just enough firewood and just enough bandboxes. This is the man's occasional glimpse and pleasing parody of thrift. But many a good housekeeper plays the same game every day with ends of cheese and scraps of silk, not because she is mean, but on the contrary, because she is magnanimous; because she wishes her creative mercy to be over all her works, that not one sardine should be destroyed, or cast as rubbish to the void, when she has made the pile complete.

The modern world must somehow be made to understand (in theology and other things) that a view may be vast, broad, universal, liberal and yet come into conflict with another view that is vast, broad, universal and liberal also. There is never a war between two sects, but only between two universal Catholic Churches. The only possible collision is the collision of one cosmos with another. So in a smaller way it must be first made clear that this female economic ideal is a part of that female variety of outlook and all-round art of life which we have already attributed to the sex. Thrift is not a small or timid or provincial thing; it is part of that great idea of the woman watching on all sides out of all the windows of the soul and being answerable for everything. For in the average human house there is one hole by which money comes in and a hundred by which it goes out; man has to do with the one hole, woman with the hundred. But though the very stinginess of a woman is a part of her spiritual breadth, it is none the less true that it brings her into conflict with the special kind of spiritual breadth that belongs to the males of the tribe. It brings her into conflict with that shapeless cataract of Comradeship, of chaotic feasting and deafening debate, which we noted in the last section. The very touch of the eternal in the two sexual tastes brings them the more into antagonism; for one stands for a universal vigilance and the other for an almost infinite output. Partly through the nature of his moral weakness, and partly through the nature of his physical strength, the male is normally prone to expand things into a sort of eternity; he always thinks of a dinner party as lasting all night; and he always thinks of a night as lasting for ever. When the working women in the poor districts come to the doors of the public houses and try to get their husbands home, simple-minded "social workers" always imagine that every husband is a tragic drunkard and every wife a broken-hearted saint. It never occurs to them that the poor woman is only doing under coarser conventions exactly what every fashionable hostess does when she tries to get the men from arguing over the cigars to come and gossip over the teacups. These women are not exasperated merely at the amount of money that is wasted in beer; they are exasperated also at the amount of time that is wasted in talk. It is not merely what goeth into the mouth but what cometh out of the mouth that, in their opinion, defileth a man. They will raise against an argument (like their sisters of all ranks) the ridiculous objection that nobody is convinced by it; as if a man wanted to make a body-slave of anybody with whom he had played single-stick. But the real female prejudice on this point is not without a basis; the real feeling is this, that the most masculine pleasures have a quality of the ephemeral. A duchess may ruin a duke for a diamond necklace; but there is the necklace. A coster may ruin his wife for a pot of beer; and where is the beer? The duchess quarrels with another duchess in order to crush her, to produce a result; the coster does not argue with another coster in order to convince him, but in order to enjoy at once the sound of his own voice, the clearness of his own opinions and the sense of masculine society. There is this element of a fine fruitlessness about the male enjoyments; wine is poured into a bottomless bucket; thought plunges into a bottomless abyss. All this has set woman against the Public House—that is, against the Parliament House. She is there to prevent waste; and the "pub" and the parliament are the very palaces of waste. In the upper classes the "pub" is called the club, but that makes no more difference to the reason than it does to the rhyme. High and low, the woman's objection to the Public House is perfectly definite and rational; it is that the Public House wastes the energies that could be used on the private house.

As it is about feminine thrift against masculine waste, so it is about feminine dignity against masculine rowdiness. The woman has a fixed and very well founded idea that if she does not insist on good manners nobody else will. Babies are not always strong on the point of dignity, and grown-up men are quite unpresentable. It is true that there are many very polite men, but none that I ever heard of who were not either fascinating women or obeying them. But indeed the female ideal of dignity, like the female ideal of thrift, lies deeper and may easily be misunderstood. It rests ultimately on a strong idea of spiritual isolation; the same that makes women religious. They do not like being melted down; they dislike and avoid the mob. That anonymous quality we have remarked in the club conversation would be common impertinence in a case of ladies. I remember an artistic and eager lady asking me in her grand green drawing-room whether I believed in comradeship between the sexes, and why not. I was driven back on offering the obvious and sincere answer "Because if I were to treat you for two minutes like a comrade you would turn me out of the house." The only certain rule on this subject is always to deal with woman and never with women. "Women" is a profligate word; I have used it repeatedly in this chapter; but it always has a blackguard sound. It smells of Oriental cynicism and hedonism. Every woman is a captive queen. But every crowd of women is only a harem broken loose.

I am not expressing my own views here, but those of nearly all the women I have known. It is quite unfair to say that a woman hates other women individually; but I think it would be quite true to say that she detests them in a confused heap. And this is not because she despises her own sex, but because she respects it; and respects especially that sanctity and separation of each item which is represented in manners by the idea of dignity and in morals by the idea of chastity.

Chapter Five

THE COLDNESS OF CHLOE

WE hear much of the human error which accepts what is sham as what is real. But it is worth while to remember that with unfamiliar things we often mistake what is real for what is sham. It is true that a very young man may think the wig of an actress is her hair. But it is equally true that a child yet younger may call the hair of a Negro his wig. Just because the woolly savage is remote and barbaric he seems to be unnaturally neat and tidy. Everyone must have noticed the same thing in the fixed and almost offensive colour of all unfamiliar things, tropic birds and tropic blossoms. Tropic birds look like staring toys out of a toy-shop. Tropic flowers simply look like artificial flowers, like things cut out of wax. This is a deep matter, and, I think, not unconnected with divinity; but anyhow it is the truth that when we see things for the first time we feel instantly that they are fictive creations; we feel the finger of God. It is only when we are thoroughly used to them and our five wits are wearied that we see them as wild and objectless; like the shapeless tree-tops or the shifting cloud. It is the design in Nature that strikes us first; the sense of the crosses and confusions in that design only comes afterwards through experience and an almost eerie monotony. If a man saw the stars abruptly by accident he would think them as festive and as artificial as a firework. We talk of the folly of painting the lily; but if we saw the lily without warning we should think that it was painted. We talk of the devil not being so black as he is painted; but that very phrase is a testimony to the kinship between what is called vivid and what is called artificial. If the modern sage had only one glimpse of grass and sky, he would say that grass was not as green as it was painted; that sky was not as blue as it was painted. If one could see the whole universe suddenly, it would look like a bright-coloured toy, just as the South American hornbill looks like a bright-coloured toy. And so they are—both of them, I mean.

But it was not with this aspect of the startling air of artifice about all strange objects that I meant to deal. I mean merely, as a guide to history, that we should not be surprised if things wrought in fashions remote from ours seem artificial; we should convince ourselves that nine times out of ten these things are nakedly and almost indecently honest. You will hear men talk of the frosted classicism of Corneille or of the powdered pomposities of the eighteenth century; but all these phrases are very superficial. There never was an artificial epoch. There never was an age of reason. Men were always men and women women: and their two generous appetites always were the expression of passion and the telling of truth. We can see something stiff and quaint in their mode of expression, just as our descendants will see something stiff and quaint in our coarsest slum sketch or our most naked pathological play. But men have never talked about anything but important things; and the next force in femininity which we have to consider can be considered best perhaps in some dusty old volume of verses by a person of quality.

The eighteenth century is spoken of as the period of artificiality, in externals at least; but, indeed, there may be two words about that. In modern speech one uses artificiality as meaning indefinitely a sort of deceit; and the eighteenth century was far too artificial to deceive. It cultivated that completest art that does not conceal the art. Its fashions and costumes positively revealed nature by avowing artifice; as in that obvious instance of a barbering that frosted every head with the same silver. It would be fantastic to call this a quaint humility that concealed youth; but, at least, it was not one with the evil pride that conceals old age. Under the eighteenth-century fashion people did not so much all pretend to be young, as all agree to be old. The same applies to the most odd and unnatural of their fashions; they were freakish, but they were not false. A lady may or may not be as red as she is painted, but plainly she was not so black as she was patched.

But I only introduce the reader into this atmosphere of the older and franker fictions that he may be induced to have patience for a moment with a certain element which is very common in the decoration and literature of that age and of the two centuries preceding it. It is necessary to mention it in such a connection because it is exactly one of those things that look as superficial as powder, and are really as rooted as hair.

In all the old flowery and pastoral love-songs, those of the seventeenth and eighteenth centuries especially, you will find a perpetual reproach against woman in the matter of her coldness; ceaseless and stale similes that compare her eyes to northern stars, her heart to ice, or her bosom to snow. Now most of us have always supposed these old and iterant phrases to be a mere pattern of dead words, a thing like a cold wall-paper. Yet I think those old cavalier poets who wrote about the coldness of Chloe had hold of a psychological truth missed in nearly all the realistic novels of to-day. Our psychological romancers perpetually represent wives as striking terror into their husbands by rolling on the floor, gnashing their teeth, throwing about the furniture or poisoning the coffee; all this upon some strange fixed theory that women are what they call emotional. But in truth the old and frigid form is much nearer to the vital fact. Most men, if they spoke with any sincerity, would agree that the most terrible quality in women was not so much being emotional as being unemotional.

There is an awful armour of ice which may be the legitimate protection of a more delicate organism; but whatever be the psychological explanation there can surely be no question of the fact. The instinctive cry of the female in anger is the *noli me tangere*. I take this as the most obvious and at the same time the least hackneyed instance of a fundamental quality in the female tradition, which has tended in our time to be almost immeasurably misunderstood, both by the cant of moralists and the cant of immoralists. The proper name for the thing is modesty; but as we live in an age of prejudice and must not call things by their right names, we will yield to a more modern nomenclature and call it dignity. Whatever else it is, it is the thing which a thousand poets and a million lovers have called the coldness of Chloe. It is akin to the classical, and is at least the opposite of the grotesque. And since we are talking here chiefly in types and symbols, perhaps as good an embodiment as any of the idea may be found in the mere fact of a woman wearing a skirt. It is highly typical of the rabid plagiarism which now passes everywhere for emancipation, that a little while ago it was common for an "advanced" woman to claim the right to wear trousers; a right about as grotesque as the right to wear a false nose. Whether female liberty is much advanced by the act of wearing a skirt on each leg I do not know; perhaps Turkish women might offer some information on the point. But if the Western woman walks about (as it were) trailing the curtains of the harem with her, it is quite certain that the woven mansion is meant for a perambulating palace, not for a perambulating prison. It is quite certain that the skirt means female dignity, not female submission; it can be proved by the simplest of all tests. No ruler would deliberately dress up in the recognised fetters of a slave; no judge would appear covered with broad arrows. But when men wish to be stately, impressive, as judges, priests or kings, they do wear skirts, the long, trailing robes of female dignity. The whole world is under petticoat government; for even men wear petticoats when they wish to govern.

Chapter Six

THE PEDANT AND THE SAVAGE

WE say then that the female holds up with two strong arms
these two pillars of civilisation; we say also that she could do
neither but for her position; her curious position of private
omnipotence, universality on a small scale. The first element
is thrift; not the destructive thrift of the miser, but the creative thrift of the peasant; the second element is dignity,
which is but the expression of sacred personality and pri-
vacy. Now I know the question that will be abruptly and
automatically asked by all that know the dull tricks and
turns of the modern sexual quarrel. The advanced person
will at once begin to argue about whether these instincts are
inherent and inevitable in woman or whether they are
merely prejudices produced by her history and education.
Now I do not propose to discuss whether woman could now
be educated out of her habits touching thrift and dignity;
and that for two excellent reasons. First it is a question
which cannot conceivably ever find any answer: that is why
modern people are so fond of it. From the nature of the case
it is obviously impossible to decide whether any of the peculiarities of civilised man have been strictly necessary to his
civilization. It is not self-evident (for instance), that even

the habit of standing upright was the only path of human progress. There might have been a quadrupedal civilisation, in which a city gentleman put on four boots to go to the city every morning. Or there might have been reptilian civilisation, in which he rolled up to the office on his stomach; it is impossible to say that intelligence might not have developed in such creatures. All we can say is that man as he is walks upright; and that woman is something almost more upright than uprightness.

And the second point is this; that upon the whole we rather prefer women (nay, even men) to walk upright; so we do not waste much of our noble lives in inventing any other way for them to walk. In short, my second reason for not speculating upon whether woman might get rid of these peculiarities, is that I do not want her to get rid of them; nor does she. I will not exhaust my intelligence by inventing ways in which mankind might unlearn the violin or forget how to ride horses; and the art of domesticity seems to me as special and as valuable as all the ancient arts of our race. Nor do I propose to enter at all into those formless and floundering speculations about how woman was or is regarded in the primitive times that we cannot remember, or in the savage countries which we cannot understand. Even if these people segregated their women for low or barbaric reasons it would not make our reasons barbaric; and I am haunted with a tenacious suspicion that these people's feelings were really, under other forms, very much the same as ours. Some impatient trader, some superficial missionary, walks across an island and sees the squaw digging in the fields while the man is playing a flute; and immediately says that the man is a mere lord of creation and the woman a mere serf. He does not remember that he might see the same thing in half the back gardens in Brixton, merely because women are at once more conscientious and more impatient, while men are at once more quiescent and more greedy for pleasure. It may often be in Hawaii simply as it is in Hoxton. That is, the woman does not work because the man tells her to work and she obeys. On the contrary, the woman works because she has told the man to work, and he hasn't obeyed. I do not affirm that this is the whole truth, but I do affirm that we have too little comprehension of the souls of savages to know how far it is untrue. It is the same with the relations of our hasty and surface science with the problem of sexual dignity and modesty. Professors find all over the world fragmentary ceremonies in which the bride affects some sort of reluctance, hides from her husband, or runs away from him. The professor then pompously proclaims that this is a survival of Marriage by Capture. I wonder he never says that the veil thrown over the bride is really a net. I gravely doubt whether women ever were married by capture. I think they pretended to be; as they do still.

It is equally obvious that these two necessary sanctities of thrift and dignity are bound to come into collision with the wordiness, the wastefulness, and the perpetual pleasure-seeking of masculine companionship. Wise women allow for the thing; foolish women try to crush it; but all women try to counteract it, and they do well. In many a home all round us at this moment we know that the nursery rhyme is reversed. The queen is in the counting-house, counting out the money. The king is in the parlour, eating bread and honey. But it must be strictly understood that the king has captured the honey in some heroic wars. The quarrel can be found in mouldering Gothic carvings and in crabbed Greek manuscripts. In every age, in every land, in every tribe and village, has been waged the great sexual war be-

tween the Private House and the Public House. I have seen
a collection of mediæval English poems, divided into sections such as "Religious Carols," "Drinking Songs" and so
on; and the section headed, "Poems of Domestic Life" consisted entirely (literally entirely) of the complaints of husbands who were bullied by their wives. Though the English was archaic, the words were in many cases precisely
the same as those which I have heard in the streets and
public-houses of Battersea, protests on behalf of an extension
of time and talk, protests against the nervous impatience
and the devouring utilitarianism of the female: Such, I say,
is the quarrel; it can never be anything but a quarrel; but
the aim of all morals and all society is to keep it a lovers'
quarrel.

Chapter Seven

THE MODERN SURRENDER OF WOMAN

But in this corner called England, at this end of the century, there has happened a strange and startling thing. Openly and to all appearance, this ancestral conflict has silently and abruptly ended; one of the two sexes has suddenly yielded to the other. By the beginning of the twentieth century, within the last few years, the woman has in public surrendered to the man. She has seriously and officially owned that the man has been right all along; that the public house (or Parliament) is really more important than the private house; that politics are not (as woman had always maintained) an excuse for pots of beer, but are a sacred solemnity to which new female worshippers may kneel; that the talkative patriots in the tavern are not only admirable but enviable; that talk is not a waste of time, and therefore (as a consequence, surely) that taverns are not a waste of money. All we men had grown used to our wives and mothers, and grandmothers, and great-aunts all pouring a chorus of contempt upon our hobbies of sport, drink and party politics. And now comes Miss Pankhurst, with tears in her eyes, owning that all the women were wrong and all the men were right; humbly imploring to be admitted into so much as an outer court, from which she may catch a glimpse of those masculine merits which her sisters had so thoughtlessly scorned.

Now this development naturally perturbs and even paralyses us. Males, like females, in the course of that old fight between the public and private house, had indulged in over-statement and extravagance, feeling that they must keep up their end of the see-saw. We told our wives that Parliament had sat late on most essential business; but it never crossed our minds that our wives would believe it. We said that everyone must have a vote in the country; similarly our wives said that no one must have a pipe in the drawing-room. In both cases the idea was the same. "It does not matter much, but if you let those things slide there is chaos." We said that Lord Huggins or Mr. Buggins was absolutely necessary to the country. We knew quite well that nothing is necessary to the country except that the men should be men and the women women. We knew this; we thought the women knew it even more clearly; and we thought the women would say it. Suddenly, without warning, the women have begun to say all the nonsense that we ourselves hardly believed when we said it. The solemnity of politics; the necessity of votes; the necessity of Huggins; the necessity of Buggins; all these flow in a pellucid stream from the lips of all the suffragette speakers. I suppose in every fight, however old, one has a vague aspiration to conquer; but we never wanted to conquer women so completely as this. We only expected that they might leave us a little more margin for our nonsense; we never expected that they would accept it seriously as sense. Therefore I am all at sea about the existing situation; I scarcely know whether to be relieved or enraged by this substitution of the feeble platform lecture for the forcible curtain-lecture. I am lost without the trenchant and candid Mrs. Caudle. I really do not know what to do with the prostrate and penitent Miss Pankhurst. This surrender of the modern woman has taken us all so much by surprise, that it is desirable to pause a moment, and collect our wits about what she is really saying.

As I have already remarked, there is one very simple answer to all this; these are not the modern women, but about one in two thousand of the modern women. This fact is important to a democrat; but it is of very little importance to the typically modern mind. Both the characteristic modern parties believe in a government by the few; the only difference is whether it is the Conservative few or Progressive few. It might be put, somewhat coarsely perhaps, by saying that one believes in any minority that is rich and the other in any minority that is mad. But in this state of things the democratic argument obviously falls out for the moment; and we are bound to take the prominent minority, merely because it is prominent. Let us eliminate altogether from our minds the thousands of women who detest this cause, and the millions of women who have hardly heard of it. Let us concede that the English people itself is not, and will not be for a very long time, within the sphere of practical politics. Let us confine ourselves to saying that these particular women want a vote and to asking ourselves what a vote is. If we ask these ladies themselves what a vote is, we shall get a very vague reply. It is the only question, as a rule, for which they are not prepared. For the truth is, that they go mainly by precedent; by the mere fact that men have votes already. So far from being a mutinous movement, it is really a very Conservative one; it is in the narrowest rut of the British Constitution. Let us take a little wider and freer sweep of thought and ask ourselves what is the ultimate point and meaning of this odd business called voting.

Chapter Eight

THE BRAND OF THE FLEUR DE LYS

SEEMINGLY from the dawn of man all nations have had governments; and all nations have been ashamed of them. Nothing is more openly fallacious than to fancy that in ruder or simpler ages ruling, judging and punishing, appeared perfectly innocent and dignified. These things were always regarded as the penalties of the Fall; as part of the humiliation of mankind, as bad in themselves. That the king can do no wrong was never anything but a legal fiction; and it is legal fiction still. The doctrine of Divine Right was not a piece of idealism, but rather a piece of realism, a practical way of ruling amid the ruin of humanity; a very pragmatist piece of faith. The religious basis of government was not so much that people put their trust in princes, as that they did not put their trust in any child of man. It was so with all the ugly institutions which disfigure human history. Torture and slavery were never talked of as good things; they were always talked of as necessary evils. A pagan spoke of one man owning ten slaves just as a modern business man speaks of one merchant sacking ten clerks; "It's very horrible; but how else can society be conducted?" A mediæval scholastic regarded the possibility of a man being burned to death just as

a modern business man regards the possibility of a man
being starved to death; "It is a shocking torture; but can
you organise a painless world?" It is possible that a future
society may find a way of doing without the question by
hunger as we have done without the question by fire. It is
equally possible, for the matter of that, that a future society
may re-establish legal torture with the whole apparatus of
rack and faggot. The most modern of countries, America,
has introduced with a vague savour of science, a method
which it calls "the third degree." This is simply the extortion
of secrets by nervous fatigue; which is surely uncommonly
close to their extortion by bodily pain. And this is legal and
scientific America. Amateur ordinary America, of course,
simply burns people alive in broad daylight, as they did in
the Reformation Wars. But though some punishments are
more inhuman than others there is no such thing as humane
punishment. As long as nineteen men claim the right in any
sense or shape to take hold of the twentieth man and make
him even mildly uncomfortable, so long the whole proceeding must be a humiliating one for all concerned. And the
proof of how poignantly men have always felt this lies in the
fact that the headsman and the hangman, the gaolers and
the torturers, were always regarded not merely with fear but
with contempt; while all kinds of careless smiters, bankrupt
knights and swashbucklers and outlaws, were regarded with
indulgence or even admiration. To kill a man lawlessly was
pardoned. To kill a man lawfully was unpardonable. The
most bare-faced duellist might almost brandish his weapon.
But the executioner was always masked.

This is the first essential element in government; coercion;
a necessary but not a noble element. I may remark in passing that when people say that government rests on force they
give an admirable instance of the foggy and muddled cyni-

cisms of modernity. Government does not rest on force. Government is force; it rests on consent or a conception of justice. A king or a community holding a certain thing to be abnormal, evil, uses the general strength to crush it out; the strength is his tool, but the belief is his only sanction. You might as well say that glass is the real reason for telescopes. But arising from whatever reason the act of government is coercive and is burdened with all the coarse and painful qualities of coercion. And if anyone asks what is the use of insisting on the ugliness of this task of state violence since all mankind is condemned to employ it, I have a simple answer to that. It would be useless to insist on it if all humanity were condemned to it. But it is not irrelevant to insist on its ugliness so long as half of humanity is kept out of it.

All government then is coercive; we happen to have created a government which is not only coercive, but collective. There are only two kinds of government, as I have already said, the despotic and the democratic. Aristocracy is not a government, it is a riot; that most effective kind of riot, a riot of the rich. The most intelligent apologists of aristocracy, sophists like Disraeli and Nietzsche, have never claimed for aristocracy any virtues but the virtues of a riot, the accidental virtues, courage, variety and adventure. There is no case anywhere of aristocracy having established a universal and applicable order, as despots and democracies have often done; as the last Cæsars created the Roman law, as the last Jacobins created the Code Napoleon. With the first of these elementary forms of government, that of the king or chieftain, we are not in this matter of the sexes immediately concerned. We shall return to it later when we remark how differently mankind has dealt with female claims in the despotic as against the democratic field.

But for the moment the essential point is that in self-governing countries this coercion of criminals is a collective coercion. The abnormal person is theoretically thumped by a million fists and kicked by a million feet. If a man is flogged, we all flogged him; if a man is hanged, we all hanged him. That is the only possible meaning of democracy, which can give any meaning to the first two syllables and also to the last two. In this sense each citizen has the high responsibility of a rioter. Every statute is a declaration of war, to be backed by arms. Every tribunal is a revolutionary tribunal. In a republic all punishment is as sacred and solemn as lynching.

Chapter Nine

SINCERITY AND THE GALLOWS

When, therefore, it is said that the tradition against Female Suffrage keeps women out of activity, social influence and citizenship, let us a little more soberly and strictly ask ourselves what it actually does keep her out of. It does definitely keep her out of the collective act of coercion; the act of punishment by a mob. The human tradition does say that, if twenty men hang a man from a tree or a lamp-post, they shall be twenty men and not women. Now I do not think any reasonable Suffragist will deny that exclusion from this function, to say the least of it, might be maintained to be a protection as well as a veto. No candid person will wholly dismiss the proposition that the idea of having a Lord Chancellor but not a Lady Chancellor may at least be connected with the idea of having a headsman but not a headswoman, a hangman but not a hangwoman. Nor will it be adequate to answer (as is so often answered to this contention) that in modern civilisation women would not really be required to capture, to sentence or to slay; that all this is done indirectly, that specialists kill our criminals as they kill our cattle. To urge this is not to urge the reality of the vote, but to urge its unreality. Democracy was meant to be a more direct way of ruling, not a more indirect way; and if we do not feel that we are all gaolers so much the worse for us, and for the prisoners. It is really an unwomanly thing to lock up a robber or a tyrant; it ought to be no softening of the situation that the woman does not feel as if she were doing the thing that she certainly is doing. It is bad enough that men can only associate on paper who could once associate in the street; it is bad enough that men have made a vote very much of a fiction. It is much worse that a great class should claim the vote because it is a fiction, who would be sickened by it if it were a fact. If votes for women do not mean mobs for women they do not mean what they were meant to mean. A woman can make a cross on a paper as well as a man; a child could do it as well as a woman; and a chimpanzee after a few lessons could do it as well as a child. But nobody ought to regard it merely as making a cross on a paper; everyone ought to regard it as what it ultimately is, branding the fleur-de-lys, marking the broad arrow, signing the death warrant. Both men and women ought to face more fully the things they do or cause to be done; face them or leave off doing them.

On that disastrous day when public executions were abolished, private executions were renewed and ratified, perhaps for ever. Things grossly unsuited to the moral sentiment of a society cannot be safely done in broad daylight; but I see no reason why we should not still be roasting heretics alive, in a private room. It is very likely (to speak in the manner foolishly called Irish) that if there were public executions there would be no executions. The old open-air punishments, the pillory and the gibbet, at least fixed responsibility upon the law; and in actual practice they gave the mob an opportunity of throwing roses as well as rotten eggs; of crying "Hosannah" as well as "Crucify." But I do not like the public executioner being turned into the private executioner. I think it is a crooked, oriental, sinister sort of business, and smells of the harem and the divan rather than of the forum and the market place. In modern times the official has lost all the social honour and dignity of the common hangman. He is only the bearer of the bowstring.

Here, however, I suggest a plea for a brutal publicity only in order to emphasise the fact that it is this brutal publicity and nothing else from which women have been excluded. I also say it to emphasise the fact that the mere modern veiling of the brutality does not make the situation different, unless we openly say that we are giving the suffrage, not because it is power, but because it is not; or in other words, that women are not so much to vote as to play at voting. No suffragist, I suppose, will take up that position; and few suffragists will wholly deny that this human necessity of pains and penalties is an ugly, humiliating business, and that good motives as well as bad may have helped to keep women out of it. More than once I have remarked in these pages that female limitations may be the limits of a temple as well as of a prison, the disabilities of a priest not of a pariah. I noted it, I think, in the case of the pontifical feminine dress. In the same way it is not evidently irrational, if men decided that a woman, like a priest, must not be a shedder of blood.

Chapter Ten

THE HIGHER ANARCHY

BUT there is a further fact; forgotten also because we moderns forget that there is a female point of view. The woman's wisdom stands partly, not only for a wholesome hesitation about punishment, but even for a wholesome hesitation about absolute rules. There was something feminine and perversely true in that phrase of Wilde's, that people should not be treated as the rule, but all of them as exceptions. Made by a man the remark was a little effeminate; for Wilde did lack the masculine power of dogma and of democratic co-operation. But if a woman had said it it would have been simply true; a woman does treat each person as a peculiar person. In other words, she stands for Anarchy; a very ancient and arguable philosophy; not anarchy in the sense of having no customs in one's life (which is inconceivable), but anarchy in the sense of having no rules for one's mind. To her, almost certainly, are due all those working traditions that cannot be found in books, especially those of education; it was she who first gave a child a stuffed stocking for being good or stood him in the corner for being naughty. This unclassified knowledge is sometimes called rule of thumb and sometimes motherwit. The last phrase suggests the whole truth, for none ever called it fatherwit.

Now anarchy is only tact when it works badly. Tact is only anarchy when it works well. And we ought to realise that in one half of the world—the private house—it does work well. We modern men are perpetually forgetting that the case for clear rules and crude penalties is not self-evident, that there is a great deal to be said for the benevolent lawlessness of the autocrat, especially on a small scale; in short, that government is only one side of life. The other half is called Society, in which women are admittedly dominant. And they have always been ready to maintain that their kingdom is better governed than ours, because (in the logical and legal sense) it is not governed at all. "Whenever you have a real difficulty," they say, "when a boy is bumptious or an aunt is stingy, when a silly girl will marry somebody, or a wicked man won't marry somebody, all your lumbering Roman Law and British Constitution come to a standstill. A snub from a duchess or a slanging from a fishwife are much more likely to put things straight." So, at least, rang the ancient female challenge down the ages until the recent female capitulation. So streamed the red standard of the higher anarchy until Miss Pankhurst hoisted the white flag.

It must be remembered that the modern world has done deep treason to the eternal intellect by believing in the swing of the pendulum. A man must be dead before he swings. It has substituted an idea of fatalistic alternation for the mediæval freedom of the soul seeking truth. All modern thinkers are reactionaries; for their thought is always a reaction from what went before. When you meet a modern man he is always coming from a place, not going to it. Thus, mankind has in nearly all places and periods seen that there is a soul and a body as plainly as that there is a sun and moon. But because a narrow Protestant sect called Materialists declared for a short time that there was no soul, another narrow Protestant sect called Christian Science is now maintaining there there is no body. Now just in the same way the unreasonable neglect of government by the Manchester School has produced, not a reasonable regard for government, but an unreasonable neglect of everything else. So that to hear people talk to-day one would fancy that every important human function must be organised and avenged by law; that all education must be state education, and all employment state employment; that everybody and everything must be brought to the foot of the august and prehistoric gibbet. But a somewhat more liberal and sympathetic examination of mankind will convince us that the cross is even older than the gibbet, that voluntary suffering was before and independent of compulsory; and in short, that in most important matters a man has always been free to ruin himself if he chose. The huge fundamental function upon which all anthropology turns, that of sex and childbirth, has never been inside the political state but always outside it. The state concerned itself with the trivial question of killing people, but wisely left alone the whole business of getting them born. A Eugenist might indeed plausibly say that the government is an absentminded and inconsistent person who occupies himself with providing for the old age of people who have never been infants. I will not deal here in any detail with the fact that some Eugenists have in our time made the maniacal answer that the police ought to control marriage and birth as they control labour and death. Except for this inhuman handful (with whom I regret to say I shall have to deal later) all the Eugenists I know divide themselves into two sections: ingenious people who once meant this, and rather bewildered people who swear they never meant it—nor anything else. But if it be conceded (by a breezier estimate of men) that they do mostly desire marriage to remain free from government, it does not follow that they desire it to remain free from everything. If man does not control the marriage market by law, is it controlled at all? Surely the answer is broadly that man does not control the marriage market by law, but that woman does control it by sympathy and prejudice. There was until lately a law forbidding a man to marry his deceased wife's sister; yet the thing happened constantly. There was no law forbidding a man to marry his deceased wife's scullerymaid; yet it did not happen nearly so often. It did not happen because the marriage market is managed in the spirit and by the authority of women; and women are generally conservative where classes are concerned. It is the same with that system of exclusiveness by which ladies have so often contrived (as by a process of elimination) to prevent the marriages that they did not want and even sometimes to procure those that they did. There is no need of the broad arrow and the *fleur-de-lys*, the turnkey's chains or the hangman's halter. You need not strangle a man if you can silence him. The branded shoulder is less effective and final than the cold shoulder; and you need not trouble to lock a man in when you can lock him out.

The same, of course, is true of the colossal architecture which we call infant education: an architecture reared wholly by women. Nothing can ever overcome that one enormous sex superiority, that even the male child is born closer to his mother than to his father. No one, staring at that frightful female privilege, can quite believe in the equality of the sexes. Here and there we read of a girl brought up like a tom-boy; but every boy is brought up like a tame girl. The flesh and spirit of femininity surround him from the first like the four walls of a house; and even the vaguest or most brutal man has been womanised by being born. Man that is born of a woman has short days and full of misery; but nobody can picture the obscenity and bestial tragedy that would belong to such a monster as man that was born of a man.

Chapter Eleven

THE QUEEN AND THE SUFFRAGETTES

But, indeed, with this educational matter I must of necessity embroil myself later. The fourth section of the discussion is supposed to be about the child, but I think it will be mostly about the mother. In this place I have systematically insisted on the large part of life that is governed, not by man with his vote, but by woman with her voice, or more often, with her horrible silence. Only one thing remains to be added. In a sprawling and explanatory style has been traced out the idea that government is ultimately coercion, that coercion must mean cold definitions as well as cruel consequences, and that therefore there is something to be said for the old human habit of keeping one-half of humanity out of so harsh and dirty a business. But the case is stronger still.

Voting is not only coercion, but collective coercion. I think Queen Victoria would have been yet more popular and satisfying if she had never signed a death warrant. I think Queen Elizabeth would have stood out as more solid and splendid in history if she had not earned (among those who happen to know her history) the nickname of Bloody Bess. I think, in short, that the great historic woman is more herself when she is persuasive rather than coercive. But I feel all mankind behind me when I say that if a woman has this power it should be despotic power—not democratic power. There is a much stronger historic argument for giving Miss Pankhurst a throne than for giving her a vote. She might have a crown, or at least a coronet, like so many of her supporters; for these old powers are purely personal and therefore female. Miss Pankhurst as a despot might be as virtuous as Queen Victoria, and she certainly would find it difficult to be as wicked as Queen Bess; but the point is that, good or bad, she would be irresponsible—she would not be governed by a rule. There are only two ways of governing: by a rule and by a ruler. And it is seriously true to say of a woman, in education and domesticity, that the freedom of the autocrat appears to be necessary to her. She is never responsible until she is irresponsible. In case this sounds like an idle contradiction, I confidently appeal to the cold facts of history. Almost every despotic or oligarchic state has admitted women to its privileges. Scarcely one democratic state has ever admitted them to its rights. The reason is very simple: that something female is endangered by violence; but endangered much more by the violence of the crowd. In short, one Pankhurst is an exception, but a thousand Pankhursts are a nightmare, a Bacchic orgy, a Witches' Sabbath. For in all legends men have thought of women as sublime separately but horrible in a herd.

Chapter Twelve

THE MODERN SLAVE

Now I have only taken the test case of Female Suffrage because it is topical and concrete; it is not of great moment for me as a political proposal. I can quite imagine anyone substantially agreeing with my view of woman as universalist and autocrat in a limited area, and still thinking that she would be none the worse for a ballot paper. The real question is whether this old ideal of woman as the great amateur is admitted or not. There are many modern things which threaten it much more than suffragism; notably the increase of self-supporting women, even in the most severe or the most squalid employments. If there be something against nature in the idea of a horde of wild women governing, there is something truly intolerable in the idea of a herd of tame women being governed. And there are elements in human psychology that make this situation particularly poignant or ignominious. The ugly exactitudes of business, the bells and clocks, the fixed hours and rigid departments, were all meant for the male, who, as a rule, can only do one thing and can only with the greatest difficulty be induced to do that. If clerks do not try to shirk their work, our whole great commercial system breaks down. It *is* breaking down,

under the inroad of women who are adopting the unprece-
dented and impossible course of taking the system seriously
and doing it well. Their very efficiency is the definition of
their slavery. It is generally a very bad sign when one is
trusted very much by one's employers. And if the evasive
clerks have a look of being blackguards, the earnest ladies
are often something very like blacklegs. But the more immediate point is that the modern working woman bears a
double burden, for she endures both the grinding officialism
of the new office and the distracting scrupulosity of the old
home. Few men understand what conscientiousness is. They
understand duty, which generally means one duty; but conscientiousness is the duty of the universalist. It is limited by
no work days or holidays; it is a lawless, limitless, devouring
decorum. If women are to be subjected to the dull rule of
commerce, we must find some way of emancipating them
from the wild rule of conscience. But I rather fancy you will
find it easier to leave the conscience and knock off the commerce. As it is, the modern clerk or secretary exhausts herself to put one thing straight in the ledger and then goes
home to put everything straight in the house.

This condition (described by some as emancipated) is at
least the reverse of my ideal. I would give women, not more
rights, but more privileges. Instead of sending her to seek
such freedom as notoriously prevails in banks and factories,
I would design specially a house in which she can be free.
And with that we come to the last point of all: the point at
which we can perceive the needs of women, like the rights
of men, stopped and falsified by something which it is the
object of this book to expose.

The Feminist (which means, I think, one who dislikes the
chief feminine characteristics) has heard my loose mono-
logue, bursting all the time with one pent up protest. At this

point he will break out and say, "But what are we to do? There is modern commerce and its clerks; there is the modern family with its unmarried daughters; specialism is expected everywhere; female thrift and conscientiousness are demanded and supplied. What does it matter whether we should in the abstract prefer the old human and housekeeping woman? We might prefer the Garden of Eden. But since women have trades, they ought to have trades-unions. Since women work in factories, they ought to vote on factory Acts. If they are unmarried they must be commercial; if they are commercial they must be political. We must have new rules for a new world—even if it be not a better one." I said to a Feminist once, "The question is not whether women are good enough for votes; it is whether votes are good enough for women." He only answered, "Ah, you go and say that to the women chain-makers on Cradley Heath."

Now this is the attitude which I attack. It is the huge heresy of Precedent. It is the view that because we have got into a mess we must grow messier to suit it; that because we have taken a wrong turn some time ago we must go forward and not backwards; that because we have lost our way we must lose our map also; and because we have missed our ideal we must forget it. There are numbers of excellent people who do not think votes unfeminine; and there may be enthusiasts for our beautiful modern industry who do not think factories unfeminine. But if these things are unfeminine it is no answer to say that they fit into each other. I am not satisfied with the statement that my daughter must have unwomanly powers because she has unwomanly wrongs. Industrial soot and political printer's ink are two blacks which do not make a white. Most of the Feminists would probably agree with me that womanhood is under shameful tyranny in the shops and mills. But I want to destroy the tyranny. They want to destroy the womanhood. That is the only difference.

Whether we can recover the clear vision of woman as a tower with many windows, the fixed eternal feminine from which her sons, the specialists, go forth; whether we can preserve the tradition of a central thing which is even more human than democracy and even more practical than politics; whether, in a word, it is possible to re-establish the family, freed from the filthy cynicism and cruelty of the commercial epoch, I shall discuss in the last section of this book. But meanwhile do not talk to me about the poor chainmakers on Cradley Heath. I know all about them and what they are doing. They are engaged in a very widespread and flourishing industry of the present age. They are making chains.

PART IV.

EDUCATION: OR THE MISTAKE ABOUT THE CHILD

Chapter One

THE CALVINISM OF TO-DAY

WHEN I wrote a little volume on my friend Mr. Bernard
Shaw, it is needless to say that he reviewed it. I naturally
felt tempted to answer, and to criticise the book from the
same disinterested and impartial standpoint from which Mr.
Shaw had criticised the subject of it. I was not withheld by
any feeling that the joke was getting a little obvious; for
an obvious joke is only a successful joke; it is only the unsuccessful clowns who comfort themselves with being subtle.
The real reason why I did not answer Mr. Shaw's amusing
attack was this; that one simple phrase in it surrendered to
me all that I have ever wanted, or could want from him to
all eternity. I told Mr. Shaw (in substance) that he was a
charming and clever fellow, but a common Calvinist. He
admitted that this was true; and there (so far as I am concerned) is an end to the matter. He said that, of course, Calvin was quite right in holding that "If once a man is born it
is too late to damn or save him." That is the fundamental
and subterranean secret; that is the last lie in hell.

The difference between Puritanism and Catholicism is
not about whether some priestly word or gesture is significant and sacred. It is about whether any word or gesture is

significant and sacred. To the Catholic every other daily
act is a dramatic dedication to the service of good or of evil.
To the Calvinist no act can have that sort of solemnity,
because the person doing it has been dedicated from eternity, and is merely filling up his time until the crack of doom.
The difference is something subtler than plum-puddings or
private theatricals; the difference is that to a Christian of
my kind this short earthly life is intensely thrilling and
precious; to a Calvinist like Mr. Shaw it is confessedly auto-
matic and uninteresting. To me these three score years and
ten are the battle. To the Fabian Calvinist (by his own confession) they are only a long procession of the victors in
laurels and the vanquished in chains. To me earthly life
is the drama; to him it is the epilogue. Shavians think about
the embryo; Spiritualists about the ghost; Christians about
the man. It is as well to have these things clear.

Now all our sociology and eugenics and the rest of it are
not so much materialist as confusedly Calvinist; they are
chiefly occupied in educating the child before he exists. The
whole movement is full of a singular depression about what
one can do with the populace, combined with a strange
disembodied gaiety about what may be done with posterity.
These essential Calvinists have, indeed, abolished some of
the more liberal and universal parts of Calvinism, such as
the belief in an intellectual design or an everlasting happiness. But though Mr. Shaw and his friends admit it is a
superstition that a man is judged after death, they stick to
their central doctrine, that he is judged before he is born.

In consequence of this atmosphere of Calvinism in the
cultured world of to-day, it is apparently necessary to begin
all arguments on education with some mention of obstetrics
and the unknown world of the prenatal. All I shall have to
say, however, on heredity will be very brief, because I shall

confine myself to what is known about it, and that is very nearly nothing. It is by no means self-evident, but it is a current modern dogma, that nothing actually enters the body at birth except a life derived and compounded from the parents. There is at least quite as much to be said for the Christian theory that an element comes from God, or the Buddhist theory that such an element comes from previous existences. But this is not a religious work, and I must submit to those very narrow intellectual limits which the absence of theology always imposes. Leaving the soul on one side, let us suppose, for the sake of argument, that the human character in the first case comes wholly from parents, and then let us curtly state our knowledge, or rather our ignorance.

Chapter Two

THE TRIBAL TERROR

POPULAR science, like that of Mr. Blatchford, is in this matter as wild as old wives' tales. Mr. Blatchford, with colossal simplicity, explained to millions of clerks and working men that the mother is like a bottle of blue beads and the father like a bottle of yellow beads; and so the child is like a bottle of mixed blue beads and yellow. He might just as well have said that if the father has two legs and the mother has two legs, the child will have four legs. Obviously it is not a question of simple addition or simple division of a number of hard detached "qualities," like beads. It is an organic crisis and transformation of the most mysterious sort; so that even if the result is unavoidable, it will still be unexpected. It is not like blue beads mixed with yellow beads; it is like blue mixed with yellow; the result of which is *green,* a totally novel and unique experience, a new emotion. A man might live in a complete cosmos of blue and yellow, like the *Edinburgh Review;* a man might never have seen anything but a golden cornfield and a sapphire sky; and still he might never have had so wild a fancy as green. If you paid a sovereign for a bluebell; if you spilt the mustard on the blue-books; if you married a canary to a blue baboon; there is nothing in any of these wild weddings that contains even a hint of green. Green is not a mental combination, like addition; it is a physical result, like birth. So apart from the fact that nobody ever really understands parents or children either, yet even if we could understand the parents we could not make any conjecture about the children. Each time the force works in a different way; each time the constituent colours combine into a different spectacle. A girl may actually inherit her ugliness from her mother's good looks. A boy may actually get his weakness from his father's strength. Even if we admit it is really a fate, for us it must remain a fairy tale. Considered in regard to its causes, the Calvinists and materialists may be right or wrong; we leave them their dreary debate. But considered in regard to its results there is no doubt about it. The thing is always a new colour; a strange star. Every birth is as lonely as a miracle. Every child is as uninvited as a monstrosity.

On all such subjects there is no science, but only a sort of ardent ignorance; and nobody has ever been able to offer any theories of moral heredity which justified themselves in the only scientific sense; that is, that one could calculate on them beforehand. There are six cases, say, of a grandson having the same twitch of mouth or vice of character as his grandfather; or perhaps there are sixteen cases, or perhaps sixty. But there are not two cases, there is not one case, there are no cases at all, of anybody betting half a crown that the grandfather will have a grandson with the twitch or the vice. In short, we deal with heredity as we deal with omens, affinities and the fulfilment of dreams. The things do happen, and when they happen we record them; but not even a lunatic ever reckons on them. Indeed, heredity, like the dreams and omens, is a barbaric notion: that is, not necessarily an untrue, but a dim, groping and unsystematised notion. A civilised man feels himself a little more free from his family. Before Christianity these tales of tribal doom occupied the savage North; and since the Reformation and the revolt against Christianity (which is the religion of a civilised freedom) savagery is slowly creeping back in the form of realistic novels and problem plays. The curse of Rougon-Macquart is as heathen and superstitious as the curse of Ravenswood; only not so well written. But in this twilight barbaric sense the feeling of a racial fate is not irrational, and may be allowed, like a hundred other half emotions that make life whole. The only essential of tragedy is that one should take it lightly. But even when the barbarian deluge rose to its highest in the madder novels of Zola (such as that called "The Human Beast"; a gross libel on beasts as well as humanity), even then the application of the hereditary idea to practice is avowedly timid and fumbling. The students of heredity are savages in this vital sense; that they stare back at marvels, but they dare not stare forward to schemes. In practice no one is mad enough to legislate or educate upon dogmas of physical inheritance; and even the language of the thing is rarely used except for special modern purposes, such as the endowment of research or the the oppression of the poor.

Chapter Three

THE TRICKS OF ENVIRONMENT

AFTER all the modern clatter of Calvinism therefore, it is only with the born child that anybody dares to deal; and the question is not eugenics but education. Or again, to adopt that rather tiresome terminology of popular science, it is not a question of heredity but of environment. I will not needlessly complicate this question by urging at length that environment also is open to some of the objections and hesitations which paralyse the employment of heredity. I will merely suggest in passing that even about the effect of environment modern people talk much too cheerfully and cheaply. The idea that surroundings will mould a man is always mixed up with the totally different idea that they will mould him in one particular way. To take the broadest case, landscape no doubt affects the soul; but how it affects it is quite another matter. To be born among pine-trees might mean loving pine-trees. It might mean loathing pine-trees. It might quite seriously mean never having seen a pine-tree. Or it might mean any mixture of these or any degree of any of them. So that the scientific method here lacks a little in precision. I am not speaking without the book; on the contrary, I am speaking with the blue-book, with the guidebook and the atlas. It may be that the Highlanders are poetical because they inhabit mountains; but are the Swiss prosaic because they inhabit mountains? It may be the Swiss have fought for freedom because they had hills; did the Dutch fight for freedom because they hadn't? Personally I should think it quite likely. Environment might work negatively as well as positively. The Swiss may be sensible, not in spite of their wild skyline, but because of their wild skyline. The Flemings may be fantastic artists, not in spite of their dull skyline, but because of it.

I only pause on this parenthesis to show that, even in matters admittedly within its range, popular science goes a great deal too fast and drops enormous links of logic. Nevertheless it remains the working reality that what we have to deal with in the case of children is, for all practical purposes, environment; or to use the older word, education. When all such deductions are made, education is at least a form of will-worship, not of cowardly fact-worship; it deals with a department that we can control; it does not merely darken us with the barbarian pessimism of Zola and the heredity-hunt. We shall certainly make fools of ourselves; that is what is meant by philosophy. But we shall not merely make beasts of ourselves; which is the nearest popular definition for merely following the laws of Nature and cowering under the vengeance of the flesh. Education contains much moonshine, but not of the sort that makes mere moon-calves and idiots, the slaves of a silver magnet, the one eye of the world. In this decent arena there are fads, but not frenzies. Doubtless we shall often find a mare's nest; but it will not always be the nightmare's.

Chapter Four

THE TRUTH ABOUT EDUCATION

WHEN a man is asked to write down what he really thinks on education a certain gravity grips and stiffens his soul, which might be mistaken by the superficial for disgust. If it be really true that men sickened of sacred words and wearied of theology, if this largely unreasoning irritation against "dogma" did arise out of some ridiculous excess of such things among priests in the past, then I fancy we must be laying up a fine crop of cant for our descendants to grow tired of. Probably the word "education" will some day seem honestly as old and objectless as the word "justification" now seems in a Puritan folio. Gibbon thought it frightfully funny that people should have fought about the difference between the "Homoousian" and the "Homoiousian." The time will come when somebody will laugh louder to think that men thundered against Sectarian Education and also against Secular Education; that men of prominence and position actually denounced the schools for teaching a creed and also for not teaching a faith. The two Greek words in Gibbon look rather alike; but they really mean quite different things. Faith and creed do not look alike, but they mean

exactly the same thing. Creed happens to be the Latin for
faith.

Now having read numberless newspaper articles on
education, and even written a good many of them, and
having heard deafening and indeterminate discussion going
on all round me almost ever since I was born, about whether
religion was a part of education, about whether hygiene was
an essential of education, about whether militarism was inconsistent with true education, I naturally pondered much
on this recurring substantive, and I am ashamed to say that
it was comparatively late in life that I saw the main fact
about it.

Of course, the main fact about education is that there is
no such thing. It does not exist, as theology or soldiering
exist. Theology is a word like geology, soldiering is a word
like smoldering; these sciences may be healthy or not as hobbies; but they deal with stones and kettles, with definite
things. But education is not a word like geology or kettles.
Education is a word like "transmission" or "inheritance"; it is
not an object, but a method. It must mean the conveying of
certain facts, views, or qualities to the last baby born. They
might be the most trivial facts, or the most preposterous
views, or the most offensive qualities; but if they are handed
on from one generation to another they are education. Education is not a thing like theology; it is not an inferior or
superior thing; it is not a thing in the same category of terms.
Theology and education are to each other as a love-letter to
the General Post Office. Mr. Fagin was quite as educational
as Dr. Strong; in practice probably more educational. It is
giving something—perhaps poison. Education is tradition,
and tradition (as its name implies) can be treason.

This first truth is frankly banal; but it is so perpetually
ignored in our political prosing that it must be made plain. A

little boy in a little house, son of a little tradesman, is taught to eat his breakfast, to take his medicine, to love his country, to say his prayers, and to wear his Sunday clothes. Obviously Fagin, if he found such a boy, would teach him to drink gin, to lie, to betray his country, to blaspheme and to wear false whiskers. But so also Mr. Salt the vegetarian would abolish the boy's breakfast; Mrs. Eddy would throw away his medicine; Count Tolstoy would rebuke him for loving his country; Mr. Blatchford would stop his prayers; and Mr. Edward Carpenter would theoretically denounce Sunday clothes, and perhaps all clothes. I do not defend any of these advanced views, not even Fagin's. But I do ask what, between the lot of them, has become of the solid entity called education. It is not (as commonly supposed) that the tradesman teaches education plus Christianity; Mr. Salt, education plus vegetarianism; Fagin, education plus crime. The truth is, that there is nothing in common at all between these teachers, except that they teach. In short, the only thing they share is the one thing they profess to dislike; the general idea of authority. It is quaint that people talk of separating dogma from education. Dogma is actually the only thing that cannot be separated from education. It *is* education. A teacher who is not dogmatic is simply a teacher who is not teaching.

Chapter Five

AN EVIL CRY

THE fashionable fallacy is that by education we can give people something that we have not got. To hear people talk one would think it was some sort of magic chemistry, by which, out of a laborious hotchpotch of hygienic meals, baths, breathing exercises, fresh air and freehand drawing, we can produce something splendid by accident; we can create what we cannot conceive. These pages have, of course, no other general purpose than to point out that we cannot create anything good until we have conceived it. It is odd that these people, who in the matter of heredity are so sullenly attached to law, in the matter of environment seem almost to believe in miracle. They insist that nothing but what was in the bodies of the parents can go to make the bodies of the children. But they seem somehow to think that things can get into the heads of the children which were not in the heads of the parents, or, indeed, anywhere else.

There has arisen in this connection a foolish and wicked cry typical of the confusion. I mean the cry called "Save the children." It is, of course, part of that modern morbidity that insists on treating the State (which is the home of man) as a sort of desperate expedient in time of panic. This

terrified opportunism is also the origin of the Socialist and
other schemes. Just as they would collect and share all the
food as men do in a famine; so they would divide the children from their fathers, as men do in a shipwreck. That a
human community might conceivably not be in a condition
of famine or shipwreck never seems to cross their minds.
This cry of "Save the children" has in it the hateful implication that it is impossible to save the fathers; in other words,
that many millions of grown up, sane, responsible and self-
supporting Europeans are to be treated as dirt or debris
and swept away out of the discussion; called dipsomaniacs
because they drink in public-houses instead of private
houses; called unemployables because nobody knows how to
get them work; called dullards if they still adhere to conventions, and called loafers if they still love liberty. Now I am
concerned, first and last, to maintain that unless you can
save the fathers, you cannot save the children; that at present we cannot save others, for we cannot save ourselves.
We cannot teach citizenship if we are not citizens; we cannot free others if we have forgotten the appetite of freedom.
Education is only truth in a state of transmission; and how
can we pass on truth if it has never come into our hand?
Thus we find that education is of all the cases the clearest
for our general purpose. It is vain to save children; for they
cannot remain children. By hypothesis we are teaching
them to be men; and how can it be so simple to teach an
ideal manhood to others if it is so vain and hopeless to find
one for ourselves?

I know that certain crazy pedants have attempted to
counter this difficulty by maintaining that education is not instruction at all, does not teach by authority at all. They present the process as coming, not from outside, from the
teacher, but entirely from inside the boy. Education, they say,

is the Latin for leading out or drawing out the dormant faculties of each person. Somewhere far down in the dim boyish soul is a primordial yearning to learn Greek accents or to wear clean collars; and the schoolmaster only gently and tenderly liberates this imprisoned purpose. Sealed up in the newborn babe are the intrinsic secrets of how to eat asparagus and what was the date of Bannockburn. The educator only draws out the child's own unapparent love of long division; only leads out the child's own slightly veiled preference for milk pudding to tarts. I am not sure that I believe in the derivation; I have heard the disgraceful suggestion that "educator," if applied to a Roman schoolmaster, did not mean leading out young functions into freedom; but only meant taking out little boys for a walk. But I am much more certain that I do not agree with the doctrine; I think it would be about as sane to say that the baby's milk comes from the baby as to say that the baby's educational merits do. There is, indeed, in each living creature a collection of forces and functions; but education means producing these in particular shapes and training them to particular purposes, or it means nothing at all. Speaking is the most practical instance of the whole situation. You may indeed "draw out" squeals and grunts from the child by simply poking him and pulling him about, a pleasant but cruel pastime to which many psychologists are addicted. But you will wait and watch very patiently indeed before you draw the English language out of him. That you have got to put into him; and there is an end of the matter.

Chapter Six

AUTHORITY THE UNAVOIDABLE

But the important point here is only that you cannot anyhow get rid of authority in education; it is not so much (as the poor Conservatives say) that parental authority ought to be preserved, as that it cannot be destroyed. Mr. Bernard Shaw once said that he hated the idea of forming a child's mind. In that case Mr. Bernard Shaw had better hang himself; for he hates something inseparable from human life. I only mentioned *educere* and the drawing out of the faculties in order to point out that even this mental trick does not avoid the inevitable idea of parental or scholastic authority. The educator drawing out is just as arbitrary and coercive as the instructor pouring in; for he draws out what he chooses. He decides what in the child shall be developed and what shall not be developed. He does not (I suppose) draw out the neglected faculty of forgery. He does not (so far at least) lead out, with timid steps, a shy talent for torture. The only result of all this pompous and precise distinction between the educator and the instructor is that the instructor pokes where he likes and the educator pulls where he likes. Exactly the same intellectual violence is done to the creature who is poked and pulled. Now we must all accept the responsïbility of this intellectual violence. Education is violent because it is creative. It is creative because it is human. It is as ruthless as playing on the fiddle; as dogmatic as drawing a picture; as brutal as building a house. In short, it is what all human action is: it is an interference with life and growth. After that it is a trifling and even a jocular question whether we say of this tremendous tormentor, the artist Man, that he puts things into us like an apothecary, or draws things out of us like a dentist.

The point is that Man does what he likes. He claims the right to take his mother Nature under his control; he claims the right to make his child, the Superman, in his image. Once flinch from this creative authority of man, and the whole courageous raid which we call civilisation wavers and falls to pieces. Now most modern freedom is at root fear. It is not so much that we are too bold to endure rules; it is rather that we are too timid to endure responsibilities. And Mr. Shaw and such people are especially shrinking from that awful and ancestral responsibilty to which our fathers committed us when they took the wild step of becoming men. I mean the responsibility of affirming the truth of our human tradition and handing it on with a voice of authority, an unshaken voice. That is the one eternal education: to be sure enough that something is true that you dare to tell it to a child. From this high audacious duty the moderns are fleeing on every side; and the only excuse for them is (of course) that their modern philosophies are so half-baked and hypothetical that they cannot convince themselves enough to convince even a newborn babe. This, of course, is connected with the decay of democracy; and is somewhat of a separate subject. Suffice it to say here that when I say that we should instruct our children, I mean that we should do it, not that Mr. Sully or Professor Earl Barnes should do it. The trouble

in too many of our modern schools is that the State, being
controlled so specially by the few, allows cranks and experiments to go straight to the school-room when they have
never passed through the Parliament, the public house,
the private house, the church, or the marketplace. Obviously, it ought to be the oldest things that are taught to the
youngest people; the assured and experienced truths that
are put first to the baby. But in a school to-day the baby has
to submit to a system that is younger than himself. The flop-
ping infant of four actually has more experience, and has
weathered the world longer, than the dogma to which he is
made to submit. Many a school boasts of having the last
ideas in education, when it has not even the first idea; for
the first idea is that even innocence, divine as it is, may learn
something from experience. But this, as I say, is all due to
the mere fact that we are managed by a little oligarchy; my
system presupposes that men who govern themselves will
govern their children. To-day we all use Popular Education
as meaning education of the people. I wish I could use it as
meaning education by the people.

The urgent point at present is that these expansive educators do not avoid the violence of authority an inch more
than the old schoolmasters. Nay, it might be maintained
that they avoid it less. The old village schoolmaster beat a
boy for not learning grammar and sent him out into the playground to play at anything he liked; or at nothing, if he liked
that better. The modern scientific schoolmaster pursues him
into the playground and makes him play at cricket, because
exercise is so good for the health. The modern Dr. Busby
is a doctor of medicine as well as a doctor of divinity. He
may say that the good of exercise is self-evident; but *he*
must say it, and say it with authority. It cannot really be
self-evident, or it never could have been compulsory. But

this is in modern practice a very mild case. In modern practice the free educationists forbid far more things than the old-fashioned educationists. A person with a taste for paradox (if any such shameless creature could exist) might with some plausibility maintain concerning all our expansion since the failure of Luther's frank paganism and its replacement by Calvin's Puritanism, that all this expansion has not been an expansion, but the closing in of a prison, so that less and less beautiful and humane things have been permitted. The Puritans destroyed images; the Rationalists forbade fairy tales; Count Tolstoy practically issued one of his papal encyclicals against music; and I have heard of modern educationists who forbid children to play with tin soldiers. I remember a meek little madman who came up to me at some Socialist soirée or other, and asked me to use my influence (have I any influence?) against adventure stories for boys. It seems they breed an appetite for blood. But never mind that; one must keep one's temper in this madhouse. I need only insist here that these things, even if a just deprivation, are a deprivation. I do not deny that the old vetoes and punishments were often idiotic and cruel; though they are much more so in a country like England (where in practice only a rich man decrees the punishment and only a poor man receives it) than in countries with a clearer popular tradition—such as Russia. In Russia flogging is often inflicted by peasants on a peasant. In modern England flogging can only in practice be inflicted by a gentleman on a very poor man. Thus only a few days ago as I write a small boy (a son of the poor, of course) was sentenced to flogging and imprisonment for five years for having picked up a small piece of coal which the experts value at fivepence. I am entirely on the side of such liberals and humanitarians as have protested against this almost bestial ignorance about boys. But I do think it a little unfair that these humanitarians, who excuse boys for being robbers, should denounce them for playing at robbers. I do think that those who understand a guttersnipe playing with a piece of coal might, by a sudden spurt of imagination, understand him playing with a tin soldier. To sum it up in one sentence: I think my meek little madman might have understood that there is many a boy who would rather be flogged, and unjustly flogged, than have his adventure story taken away.

Chapter Seven

THE HUMILITY OF MRS. GRUNDY

In short, the new education is as harsh as the old, whether or no it is as high. The freest fad, as much as the strictest formula, is stiff with authority. It is because the humane father thinks soldiers wrong that they are forbidden; there is no pretence, there can be no pretence, that the boy would think so. The average boy's impression certainly would be simply this: "If your father is a Methodist you must not play with soldiers on Sunday. If your father is a Socialist you must not play with them even on weekdays." All education-ists are utterly dogmatic and authoritarian. You cannot have free education; for if you left a child free you would not educate him at all. Is there, then, no distinction or differ-ence between the most hide-bound conventionalists and the most brilliant and bizarre innovators? Is there no difference between the heaviest heavy father and the most reckless and speculative maiden aunt? Yes; there is. The difference is that the heavy father, in his heavy way, is a democrat. He does not urge a thing merely because to his fancy it should be done, but because (in his own admirable repub-lican formula) "Everybody does it." The conventional au-thority does claim some popular mandate; the unconven-tional authority does not. The Puritan who forbids soldiers on Sunday is at least expressing Puritan opinion; not merely his own opinion. He is not a despot; he is a democracy, a

tyrannical democracy, a dingy and local democracy perhaps;
but one that could do and has done the two ultimate virile
things—fight and appeal to God. But the veto of the new
educationist is like the veto of the House of Lords: it does
not pretend to be representative. These innovators are always talking about the blushing modesty of Mrs. Grundy. I
do not know whether Mrs. Grundy is more modest than they
are; but I am sure she is more humble.

But there is a further complication. The more anarchic
modern may again attempt to escape the dilemma by saying
that education should only be an enlargement of the mind,
an opening of all the organs of receptivity. Light (he says)
should be brought into darkness; blinded and thwarted existences in all our ugly corners should merely be permitted
to perceive and expand; in short, enlightenment should be
shed over darkest London. Now here is just the trouble:
that, in so far as this is involved, there is no darkest London.
London is not dark at all; not even at night. We have said
that if education is a solid substance, then there is none of
it. We may now say that if education is an abstract expansion, there is no lack of it. There is far too much of it. In
fact, there is nothing else.

There are no uneducated people. Everybody in England
is educated; only most people are educated wrong. The
State schools were not the first schools, but among the last
schools to be established; and London had been educating
Londoners long before the London School Board. The error
is a highly practical one. It is persistently assumed that unless a child is civilised by the established schools, he must
remain a barbarian. I wish he did. Every child in London
becomes a highly civilised person. But there are so many
different civilisations, most of them born tired. Anyone will
tell you that the trouble with the poor is not so much that

the old are still foolish, but rather that the young are already wise. Without going to school at all, the gutter-boy would be educated. Without going to school at all, he would be over-educated. The real object of our schools should be not so much to suggest complexity as solely to restore simplicity. You will hear venerable idealists declare we must make war on the ignorance of the poor; but, indeed, we have rather to make war on their knowledge. Real educationists have to resist a kind of roaring cataract of culture. The truant is being taught all day. If the children do not look at the large letters in the spelling-book, they need only walk outside and look at the large letters on the poster. If they do not care for the coloured maps provided by the school, they can gape at the coloured maps provided by the *Daily Mail*. If they tire of electricity, they can take to electric trams. If they are unmoved by music, they can take to drink. If they will not work so as to get a prize from their school, they may work to get a prize from *Prizy Bits*. If they cannot learn enough about law and citizenship to please the teacher, they learn enough about them to avoid the policeman. If they will not learn history forwards from the right end in the history books, they will learn it backwards from the wrong end in the party newspapers. And this is the tragedy of the whole affair: that the London poor, a particularly quickwitted and civilised class, learn everything tail foremost, learn even what is right in the way of what is wrong. They do not see the first principles of law in a law book; they only see its last results in the police news. They do not see the truths of politics in a general survey. They only see the lies of politics at a General Election.

But whatever be the pathos of the London poor, it has nothing to do with being uneducated. So far from being without guidance, they are guided constantly, earnestly,

excitedly; only guided wrong. The poor are not at all neglected, they are merely oppressed; nay, rather they are per-
secuted. There are no people in London who are not appealed to by the rich; the appeals of the rich shriek from
every hoarding and shout from every hustings. For it should
always be remembered that the queer, abrupt ugliness of
our streets and costumes are not the creation of democracy,
but of aristocracy. The House of Lords objected to the Em-
bankment being disfigured by trams. But most of the rich
men who disfigure the street walls with their wares are actually in the House of Lords. The peers make the country
seats beautiful by making the town streets hideous. This,
however, is parenthetical. The point is, that the poor in London are not left alone, but rather deafened and bewildered
with raucous and despotic advice. They are not like sheep
without a shepherd. They are more like one sheep whom
twenty-seven shepherds are shouting at. All the newspapers,
all the new advertisements, all the new medicines and new
theologies, all the glare and blare of the gas and brass of
modern times—it is against these that the national school
must bear up if it can. I will not question that our elementary education is better than barbaric ignorance. But there
is no barbaric ignorance. I do not doubt that our schools
would be good for uninstructed boys. But there are no uninstructed boys. A modern London school ought not merely to
be clearer, kindlier, more clever and more rapid than ignorance and darkness. It must also be clearer than a picture
postcard, cleverer than a Limerick competition, quicker
than the tram, and kindlier than the tavern. The school,
in fact, has the responsibility of universal rivalry. We need
not deny that everywhere there is a light that must conquer
darkness. But here we demand a light that can conquer
light.

Chapter Eight

THE BROKEN RAINBOW

I WILL take one case that will serve both as symbol and example; the case of colour. We hear the realists (those sentimental fellows) talking about the grey streets and the grey lives of the poor. But whatever the poor streets are they are not grey; but motley, striped, spotted, piebald and patched like a quilt. Hoxton is not æsthetic enough to be monochrome; and there is nothing of the Celtic twilight about it. As a matter of fact, a London gutter-boy walks unscathed among furnaces of colour. Watch him walk along a line of hoardings, and you will see him now against glowing green, like a traveller in a tropic forest; now black, like a bird against the burning blue of the Midi; now *passant* across a field gules, like the golden leopards of England. He ought to understand the irrational rapture of that cry of Mr. Stephen Phillips about "that bluer blue, that greener green." There is no blue much bluer than Reckitt's Blue and no blacking blacker than Day and Martin's; no more emphatic yellow than that of Colman's Mustard. If, despite this chaos of colour, like a shattered rainbow, the spirit of the small boy is not exactly intoxicated with art and culture, the cause certainly does not lie in universal greyness or the mere starving of his senses. It lies in the fact that the colours are presented in the wrong connection, on the wrong scale, and, above all, from the wrong motive. It is not colours he lacks, but a philosophy of colours. In short, there is nothing wrong with Reckitt's Blue except that it is not Reckitt's. Blue does not belong to Reckitt, but to the sky; black does not belong to Day and Martin, but to the abyss. Even the finest posters are only very little things on a very large scale. There is something specially irritant in this way about the iteration of advertisements of mustard: a condiment, a small luxury; a thing in its nature not to be taken in quantity. There is a special irony in these starving streets to see such a great deal of mustard to such very little meat. Yellow is a bright pigment; mustard is a pungent pleasure. But to look at these seas of yellow is to be like a man who should swallow gallons of mustard. He would either die, or lose the taste of mustard altogether.

Now suppose we compare these gigantic trivialities on the hoardings with those tiny and tremendous pictures in which the mediævals recorded their dreams; little pictures where the blue sky is hardly larger than a single sapphire, and the fires of judgment only a pigmy patch of gold. The difference here is not merely that poster art is in its nature more hasty than illumination art; it is not even merely that the ancient artist was serving the Lord while the modern artist is serving the lords. It is that the old artist contrived to convey an impression that colours really were significant and precious things, like jewels and talismanic stones. The colour was often arbitrary; but it was always authoritative. If a bird was blue, if a tree was golden, if a fish was silver, if a cloud was scarlet, the artist managed to convey that these colours were important and almost painfully intense: all the red red-hot and all the gold tried in the fire. Now that is the spirit touching colour which the schools must recover and protect if they are really to give the children any imaginative appetite or pleasure in the thing. It is not so much an indulgence in colour; it is rather, if anything, a sort of fiery thrift. It fenced in a green field in heraldry as straitly as a green field in peasant proprietorship. It would not fling away gold leaf any more than gold coin; it would not heedlessly pour out purple or crimson, any more than it would spill good wine or shed blameless blood. That is the hard task before educationists in this special matter; they have to teach people to relish colours like liqueurs. They have the heavy business of turning drunkards into wine tasters. If ever the twentieth century succeeds in doing this, it will almost catch up with the twelfth.

The principle covers, however, the whole of modern life. Morris and the merely æsthetic mediævalists always indicated that a crowd in the time of Chaucer would have been brightly clad and glittering, compared with a crowd in the time of Queen Victoria. I am not so sure that the real distinction is here. There would be brown frocks of friars in the first scene as well as brown bowlers of clerks in the second. There would be purple plumes of factory girls in the second scene as well as purple lenten vestments in the first. There would be white waistcoats against white ermine; gold watch chains against gold lions. The real difference is this; that the brown earth-colour of the monk's coat was instinctively chosen to express labour and humility, whereas the brown colour of the clerk's hat was not chosen to express anything. The monk did mean to say that he robed himself in dust. I am sure the clerk does not mean to say that he crowns himself with clay. He is not putting dust on his head, as the only diadem of man. Purple, at once rich and sombre, does suggest a triumph temporarily eclipsed by a tragedy. But the factory girl does not intend her hat to express a triumph temporarily eclipsed by a tragedy: far from it. White ermine was meant to express moral purity; white waistcoats were not. Gold lions do suggest a flaming magnanimity; gold watch chains do not. The point is not that we have lost the material hues, but that we have lost the trick of turning them to the best advantage. We are not like children who have lost their paint-box and are left alone with a grey lead-pencil. We are like children who have mixed all the colours in the paint-box together and lost the paper of instructions. Even then (I do not deny) one has some fun.

Now this abundance of colours and loss of a colour scheme is a pretty perfect parable of all that is wrong with our modern ideals and especially with our modern education. It is the same with ethical education, economic education, every sort of education. The growing London child will find no lack of highly controversial teachers who will teach him that geography means painting the map red; that economics means taxing the foreigner; that patriotism means the peculiarly un-English habit of flying a flag on Empire Day. In mentioning these examples specially I do not mean to imply that there are no similar crudities and popular fallacies upon the other political side. I mention them because they constitute a very special and arresting feature of the situation. I mean this, that there were always Radical revolutionists; but now there are Tory revolutionists also. The modern Conservative no longer conserves. He is avowedly an innovator. Thus all the current defences of the House of Lords which describe it as a bulwark against the mob are intellectually done for; the bottom has fallen out of them; because on five or six of the most turbulent topics of the day the House of Lords is a mob itself; and exceedingly likely to behave like one.

Chapter Nine

THE NEED FOR NARROWNESS

THROUGH all this chaos, then, we come back once more to our main conclusion. The true task of culture to-day is not a task of expansion, but very decidedly of selection—and re-jection. The educationist must find a creed and teach it. Even if it be not a theological creed, it must still be as fastidious and as firm as theology. In short, it must be ortho-dox. The teacher may think it antiquated to have to decide precisely between the faith of Calvin and of Laud, the faith of Aquinas and of Swedenborg; but he still has to choose between the faith of Kipling and of Shaw, between the world of Blatchford and of General Booth. Call it, if you will, a narrow question whether your child shall be brought up by the vicar or the minister or the popish priest. You have still to face that larger, more liberal, more highly civilised question, of whether he shall be brought up by Harmsworth or by Pearson, by Mr. Eustace Miles with his Simple Life or Mr. Peter Keary with his Strenuous Life; whether he shall most eagerly read Miss Annie S. Swan or Mr. Bart Kennedy; in short, whether he shall end up in the mere violence of the S.D.F. or in the mere vulgarity of the Primrose League. They say that nowadays the creeds are crumbling; I doubt it, but at least the sects are increasing;

and education must now be sectarian education, merely for practical purposes. Out of all this throng of theories it must somehow select a theory; out of all these thundering voices it must manage to hear a voice; out of all this awful and aching battle of blinding lights, without one shadow to give shape to them, it must manage somehow to trace and to track a star.

I have spoken so far of popular education, which began too vague and vast and which therefore has accomplished little. But as it happens there is in England something to compare it with. There is an institution, or class of institutions, which began with the same popular object, which has since followed a much narrower object; but which had the great advantage that it did follow some object, unlike our modern elementary schools.

In all these problems I should urge the solution which is positive, or, as silly people say, "optimistic." I should set my face, that is, against most of the solutions that are solely negative and abolitionist. Most educators of the poor seem to think that they have to teach the poor man not to drink. I should be quite content if they teach him to drink; for it is mere ignorance about how to drink and when to drink that is accountable for most of his tragedies. I do not propose (like some of my revolutionary friends) that we should abolish the public schools. I propose the much more lurid and desperate experiment that we should make them public. I do not wish to make Parliament stop working, but rather to make it work; not to shut up churches, but rather to open them; not to put out the lamp of learning or destroy the hedge of property; but only to make some rude effort to make universities fairly universal and property decently proper.

In many cases, let it be remembered, such action is not

merely going back to the old ideal, but is even going back
to the old reality. It would be a great step forward for the
gin shop to go back to the inn. It is incontrovertibly true that
to mediævalise the public schools would be to democratise
the public schools. Parliament did once really mean (as its
name seems to imply) a place where people were allowed
to talk. It is only lately that the general increase of efficiency,
that is of the Speaker, has made it mostly a place where
people are prevented from talking. The poor do not go to
the modern church, but they went to the ancient church all
right; and if the common man in the past had a grave respect
for property, it may conceivably have been because he sometimes had some of his own. I therefore can claim that I have
no vulgar itch of innovation in anything I say about any of
these institutions. Certainly I have none in that particular
one which I am now obliged to pick out of the list; a type
of institution to which I have genuine and personal reasons
for being friendly and grateful: I mean the great Tudor
foundations, the public schools of England. They have been
praised for a great many things, mostly, I am sorry to say,
praised by themselves and their children. And yet for some
reason no one has ever praised them for the one really
convincing reason.

Chapter Ten

THE CASE FOR THE PUBLIC SCHOOLS

THE word success can of course be used in two senses. It may be used with reference to a thing serving its immediate and peculiar purpose, as of a wheel going round; or it can be used with reference to a thing adding to the general welfare, as of a wheel being a useful discovery. It is one thing to say that Smith's flying machine is a failure, and quite another to say that Smith has failed to make a flying machine. Now this is very broadly the difference between the old English public schools and the new democratic schools. Perhaps the old public schools are (as I personally think they are) ultimately weakening the country rather than strengthening it, and are therefore, in that ultimate sense, inefficient. You can make your flying ship so that it flies, even if you also make it so that it kills you. Now the public school system may not work satisfactorily, but it works; the public schools may not achieve what we want, but they achieve what they want. The popular elementary schools do not in that sense achieve anything at all. It is very difficult to point to any guttersnipe in the street and say that he embodies the ideal for which popular education has been working, in the sense that the fresh-faced, foolish boy in "Etons" does embody the ideal for which the head-masters of Harrow and Winchester have been working. The aristocratic educationists have the positive purpose of turn-ing out gentlemen; and they do turn out gentlemen, even when they expel them. The popular educationists would say that they had the far nobler idea of turning out citizens. I concede that it is a much nobler idea, but where are the citizens? I know that the boy in "Etons" is stiff with a rather silly and sentimental stoicism, called being a man of the world. I do not fancy that the errand-boy is rigid with the republican stoicism that is called being a citizen. The schoolboy will really say with fresh and innocent *hauteur*, "I am an English gentleman." I cannot so easily picture the errand-boy drawing up his head to the stars and answering, "Romanus Civis Sum." Let it be granted that our elemen-tary teachers are teaching the very broadest code of morals, while our great headmasters are teaching only the narrowest code of manners. Let it be granted that both these things are being taught. But only one of them is being learnt.

It is always said that great reformers or masters of events can manage to bring about some specific and practical re-forms, but that they never fulfil their visions or satisfy their souls. I believe there is a real sense in which this apparent platitude is quite untrue. By a strange inversion the political idealist often does not get what he asks for, but does get what he wants. The silent pressure of his ideal lasts much longer and reshapes the world much more than the actu-alities by which he attempted to suggest it. What perishes is the letter, which he thought so practical. What endures is the spirit, which he felt to be unattainable and even unut-terable. It is exactly his schemes that are not fulfilled; it is exactly his vision that is fulfilled. Thus the ten or twelve paper constitutions of the French Revolution, which seemed so business-like to the framers of them, seem to us to have flown away on the wind as the wildest fancies. What has not flown away, what is a fixed fact in Europe, is the ideal and vision. The Republic, the idea of a land full of mere citizens all with some minimum of manners and minimum of wealth, the vision of the eighteenth century, the reality of the twentieth. So I think it will generally be with the creator of social things, desirable or undesirable. All his schemes will fail, all his tools break in his hands. His compromises will collapse, his concessions will be useless. He must brace himself to bear his fate; he shall have nothing but his heart's desire.

Now if one may compare very small things with very great, one may say that the English aristocratic schools can claim something of the same sort of success and solid splendour as the French democratic politics. At least they can claim the same sort of superiority over the distracted and fumbling attempts of modern England to establish democratic education. Such success as has attended the public schoolboy throughout the Empire, a success exaggerated indeed by himself, but still positive and a fact of a certain indisputable shape and size, has been due to the central and supreme circumstance that the managers of our public schools did know what sort of boy they liked. They wanted something and they got something; instead of going to work in the broad-minded manner and wanting everything and getting nothing.

The only thing in question is the quality of the thing they got. There is something highly maddening in the circumstance that when modern people attack an institution that really does demand reform, they always attack it for the wrong reasons. Thus many opponents of our public schools, imagining themselves to be very democratic, have exhausted themselves in an unmeaning attack upon the study of Greek. I can understand how Greek may be regarded as useless, especially by those thirsting to throw themselves into the cutthroat commerce which is the negation of citizenship; but I do not understand how it can be considered undemocratic. I quite understand why Mr. Carnegie has hatred of Greek. It is obscurely founded on the firm and sound impression that in any self-governing Greek city he would have been killed. But I cannot comprehend why any chance democrat, say Mr. Quelch, or Mr. Will Crooks, or Mr. John M. Robertson, should be opposed to people learning the Greek alphabet, which was the alphabet of liberty. Why should Radicals dislike Greek? In that language is written all the earliest and, Heaven knows, the most heroic history of the Radical party. Why should Greek disgust a democrat, when the very word democrat is Greek?

A similar mistake, though a less serious one, is merely attacking the athletics of public schools as something promoting animalism and brutality. Now brutality, in the only immoral sense, is not a vice of the English public schools. There is much moral bullying, owing to the general lack of moral courage in the public-school atmosphere. These schools do, upon the whole, encourage physical courage; but they do not merely discourage moral courage, they forbid it. The ultimate result of the thing is seen in the egregious English officer who cannot even endure to wear a bright uniform except when it is blurred and hidden in the smoke of battle. This, like all the affectations of our present plutocracy, is an entirely modern thing. It was unknown to the old aristocrats. The Black Prince would certainly have asked that any knight who had the courage to lift his crest among his enemies, should also have the courage to lift it among his friends. As regards moral courage, then, it is not so much that the public schools support it feebly, as that they suppress it firmly. But physical courage they do, on the whole, support; and physical courage is a magnificent fundamental. The one great, wise Englishman of the eighteenth century said truly that if a man lost that virtue he could never be sure of keeping any other. Now it is one of the mean and morbid modern lies that physical courage is connected with cruelty. The Tolstoyan and Kiplingite are nowhere more at one than in maintaining this. They have, I believe, some small sectarian quarrel with each other, the one saying that courage must be abandoned because it is connected with cruelty, and the other maintaining that cruelty is charming because it is a part of courage. But it is all, thank God, a lie. An energy and boldness of body may make a man stupid or reckless or dull or drunk or hungry, but it does not make him spiteful. And we may admit heartily (without joining in that perpetual praise which public school men are always pouring upon themselves) that this does operate to the removal of mere evil cruelty in the public schools. English public school life is extremely like English public life, for which it is the preparatory school. It is like it specially in this, that things are either very open, common and conventional, or else are very secret indeed. Now there is cruelty in public schools, just as there is kleptomania and secret drinking and vices without a name. But these things do not flourish in the full daylight and common consciousness of the school; and no more does cruelty. A tiny trio of sullen-looking boys gather in corners and seem to have some ugly business always; it may be indecent literature, it may be the beginning of drink, it may occasionally be cruelty to little boys. But on this stage the bully is not a braggart. The proverb says that bullies are always cowardly, but these bullies are more than cowardly, they are shy.

As a third instance of the wrong form of revolt against the public schools, I may mention the habit of using the word aristocracy with a double implication. To put the plain truth as briefly as possible, if aristocracy means rule by a rich ring, England has aristocracy and the English public schools support it. If it means rule by ancient families or flawless blood, England has not got aristocracy, and the public schools systematically destroy it. In these circles real aristocracy, like real democracy, has become bad form. A modern fashionable host dare not praise his ancestry; it would so often be an insult to half the other oligarchs at table who have no ancestry. We have said he has not the moral courage to wear his uniform; still less has he the moral courage to wear his coat-of-arms. The whole thing now is only a vague hotch-potch of nice and nasty gentlemen. The nice gentleman never refers to anyone else's father, the nasty gentleman never refers to his own. That is the only difference; the rest is the public school manner. But Eton and Harrow have to be aristocratic because they consist so largely of parvenus. The public school is not a sort of refuge for aristocrats, like an asylum, a place where they go in and never come out. It is a factory for aristocrats; they come out without ever having perceptibly gone in. The poor little private schools, in their old-world, sentimental, feudal style, used to stick up a notice "For the Sons of Gentlemen only." If the public schools stuck up a notice it ought to be inscribed "For the Fathers of Gentlemen only." In two generations they can do the trick.

Chapter Eleven

THE SCHOOL FOR HYPOCRITES

THESE are the false accusations; the accusation of classicism, the accusation of cruelty, and the accusation of an exclusiveness based on perfection of pedigree. English public school boys are not pedants, they are not torturers; and they are not, in the vast majority of cases, people fiercely proud of their ancestry, or even people with any ancestry to be proud of. They are taught to be courteous, to be good tempered, to be brave in a bodily sense, to be clean in a bodily sense; they are generally kind to animals, generally civil to servants, and to anyone in any sense their equal, the jolliest companions on earth. Is there then anything wrong in the public school ideal? I think we all feel there is something very wrong in it, but a blinding network of newspaper phraseology obscures and entangles us; so that it is hard to track to its beginning, beyond all words and phrases, the faults in this great English achievement.

Surely, when all is said, the ultimate objection to the English public school is its utterly blatant and indecent disregard of the duty of telling the truth. I know there does still linger among maiden ladies in remote country houses a notion that English schoolboys are taught to tell the truth, but it cannot be maintained seriously for a moment. Very occasionally, very vaguely, English schoolboys are told not to tell lies, which is a totally different thing. I may silently support all the obscene fictions and forgeries in the universe, without once telling a lie. I may wear another man's coat, steal another man's wit, apostatise to another man's creed, or poison another man's coffee, all without ever telling a lie. But no English schoolboy is ever taught to tell the truth, for the very simple reason that he is never taught to desire the truth. From the very first he is taught to be totally careless about whether a fact is a fact; he is taught to care only whether the fact can be used on his "side" when he is engaged in "playing the game." He takes sides in his Union debating society to settle whether Charles I ought to have been killed, with the same solemn and pompous frivolity with which he takes sides in the cricket field to decide whether Rugby or Westminster shall win. He is never allowed to admit the abstract notion of the truth, that the match is a matter of what may happen, but that Charles I is a matter of what did happen—or did not. He is Liberal or Tory at the general election exactly as he is Oxford or Cambridge at the boat-race. He knows that sport deals with the unknown; he has not even a notion that politics should deal with the known. If anyone really doubts this self-evident proposition, that the public schools definitely discourage the love of truth, there is one fact which I should think would settle him. England is the country of the Party System, and it has always been chiefly run by public school men. Is there anyone out of Hanwell who will maintain that the Party System, whatever its conveniences or inconveniences, could have been created by people particularly fond of truth?

The very English happiness on this point is itself a hypocrisy. When a man really tells the truth the first truth he tells is that he himself is a liar. David said in his haste, that is, in his honesty, that all men are liars. It was afterwards, in some leisurely official explanation, that he said that Kings of Israel at least told the truth. When Lord Curzon was Viceroy he delivered a moral lecture to the Indians on their reputed indifference to veracity, to actuality and intellectual honour. A great many people indignantly discussed whether Orientals deserved to receive this rebuke; whether Indians were indeed in a position to receive such severe admonition. No one seemed to ask, as I should venture to ask, whether Lord Curzon was in a position to give it. He is an ordinary party politician; a party politician means a politician who might have belonged to either party. Being such a person he must again and again at every twist and turn of party strategy, either have deceived others or grossly deceived himself. I do not know the East; nor do I like what I know. I am quite ready to believe that when Lord Curzon went out he found a very false atmosphere. I only say it must have been something startlingly and chokingly false if it was falser than that English atmosphere from which he came. The English Parliament actually cares for everything except veracity. The public school man is kind, courageous, polite, clean, companionable; but, in the most awful sense of the words, the truth is not in him.

This weakness of untruthfulness in the English public schools, in the English political system, and to some extent in the English character, is a weakness which necessarily produces a curious crop of superstitions, of lying legends, of evident delusions clung to through low spiritual self-indulgence. There are so many of these public school superstitions that I have here only space for one of them, which may be called the superstition of soap. It appears to have been shared by the ablutionary Pharisees, who resembled the

English public school aristocrats in so many respects: in their care about club rules and traditions, in their offensive optimism at the expense of other people, and above all in their unimaginative plodding patriotism in the worst interests of their country. Now the old human common sense about washing is that it is a great pleasure. Water (applied externally) is a splendid thing, like wine. Sybarites bathe in wine, and Nonconformists drink water; but we are not concerned with these frantic exceptions. Washing being a pleasure, it stands to reason that rich people can afford it more than poor people, and as long as this was recognised all was well; and it was very right that rich people should offer baths to poor people, as they might offer any other agreeable thing—a drink or a donkey ride. But one dreadful day, somewhere about the middle of the nineteenth century, somebody discovered (somebody pretty well off) the two great modern truths, that washing is a virtue in the rich and therefore a duty in the poor. For a duty is a virtue that one can't do. And a virtue is generally a duty that one can do quite easily; like the bodily cleanliness of the upper classes. But in the public school tradition of public life, soap has become creditable simply because it is pleasant. Baths are represented as a part of the decay of the Roman Empire; but the same baths are represented as part of the energy and rejuvenation of the British Empire. There are distinguished public schoolmen, bishops, dons, headmasters, and high politicians, who, in the course of the eulogies which from time to time they pass upon themselves, have actually identified physical cleanliness with moral purity. They say (if I remember right) that a public school man is clean inside and out. As if everyone did not know that while saints can afford to be dirty, seducers have to be clean. As if everyone did not know that the harlot must be clean, because it is her business to captivate, while the good wife may be dirty, because it is her business to clean. As if we did not all know that whenever God's thunder cracks above us, it is very likely indeed to find the simplest man in a muck cart and the most complex blackguard in a bath.

There are other instances, of course, of this oily trick of turning the pleasures of a gentleman into the virtues of an Anglo-Saxon. Sport, like soap, is an admirable thing, but like soap, it is an agreeable thing. And it does not sum up all moral merits to be a sportsman playing the game in a world where it is so often necessary to be a workman doing the work. By all means let a gentleman congratulate himself that he has not lost his natural love of pleasure, as against the *blasé* and unchildlike. But when one has the childlike joy it is best to have also the childlike unconsciousness; and I do not think we should have special affection for the little boy who everlastingly explained that it was his duty to play Hide and Seek and one of his family virtues to be prominent in Puss in the Corner.

Another such irritating hypocrisy is the oligarchic attitude towards mendicity as against organised charity. Here again, as in the case of cleanliness and of athletics, the attitude would be perfectly human and intelligible if it were not maintained as a merit. Just as the obvious thing about soap is that it is a convenience, so the obvious thing about beggars is that they are an inconvenience. The rich would deserve very little blame if they simply said that they never dealt directly with beggars, because in modern urban civilisation it is impossible to deal directly with beggars; or if not impossible at least very difficult. But these people do not refuse money to beggars on the ground that such charity is difficult. They refuse it on the grossly hypocritical ground that such charity is easy. They say, with the most grotesque gravity, "Anyone can put his hand in his pocket and give a poor man a penny; but we, we philanthropists, go home and brood and travail over the poor man's troubles until we have discovered exactly what jail, reformatory, workhouse, or lunatic asylum it will really be best for him to go to." This is all sheer lying. They do not brood about the man when they get home, and if they did it would not alter the original fact that their motive for discouraging beggars is the perfectly rational one that beggars are a bother. A man may easily be forgiven for not doing this or that incidental act of charity, especially when the question is as genuinely difficult and dubious as is the case of mendicity. But there is something quite pestilently Pecksniffian about shrinking from a hard task on the plea that it is not hard enough. If any man will really try talking to the ten beggars who come to his door he will soon find out whether it is really so much easier than the labour of writing a cheque for a hospital.

Chapter Twelve

THE STALENESS OF THE NEW SCHOOLS

FOR this deep and disabling reason therefore, its cynical and abandoned indifference to the truth, the English public school does not provide us with the ideal that we require. We can only ask its modern critics to remember that right or wrong the thing can be done; the factory is working, the wheels are going round, the gentlemen are being produced, with their soap, cricket and organised charity all complete. And in this, as we have said before, the public school really has an advantage over all the other educational schemes of our time. You can pick out a public school man in any of the many companies into which they stray, from a Chinese opium den to a German bankers' dinner-party. But I doubt if you could tell which little match girl had been brought up by Undenominational Religion and which by Secular Education. The great English aristocracy which has ruled us since the Reformation is really, in this sense, a model to the moderns. It did have an ideal, and therefore it has produced a reality.

We may repeat here that these pages propose mainly to show one thing: that progress ought to be based on principle, while our modern progress is mostly based on precedent.

We go, not by what may be affirmed in theory, but by what has been already admitted in practice. That is why the Jacobites are the last Tories in history with whom a high-spirited person can have much sympathy. They wanted a specific thing; they were ready to go forward for it, and so they were also ready to go back for it. But modern Tories have only the dullness of defending situations that they had not the excitement of creating. Revolutionists make a reform, Conservatives only conserve the reform. They never reform the reform, which is often very much wanted. Just as the rivalry of armaments is only a sort of sulky plagiarism, so the rivalry of parties is only a sort of sulky inheritance. Men have votes, so women must soon have votes; poor children are taught by force, so they must soon be fed by force; the police shut public houses by twelve o'clock, so soon they must shut them by eleven o'clock; children stop at school till they are fourteen, so soon they will stop till they are forty. No gleam of reason, no momentary return to first principles, no abstract asking of any obvious question, can interrupt this mad and monotonous gallop of mere progress by precedent. It is a good way to prevent real revolution. By this logic of events, the Radical gets as much into a rut as the Conservative. We meet one hoary old lunatic who says his grandfather told him to stand by one stile. We meet another hoary old lunatic who says his grandfather told him only to walk along one lane.

I say we may repeat here this primary part of the argument, because we have just now come to the place where it is most startlingly and strongly shown. The final proof that our elementary schools have no definite ideal of their own is the fact that they so openly imitate the ideals of the public schools. In the elementary schools we have all the ethical prejudices and exaggerations of Eton and Harrow carefully copied for people to whom they do not even roughly apply. We have the same wildly disproportionate doctrine of the effect of physical cleanliness on moral character. Educators and educational politicians declare, amid warm cheers, that cleanliness is far more important than all the squabbles about moral and religious training. It would really seem that so long as a little boy washes his hands it does not matter whether he is washing off his mother's jam or his brother's gore. We have the same grossly insincere pretence that sport always encourages a sense of honour, when we know that it often ruins it. Above all, we have the same great upper-class assumption that things are done best by large institutions handling large sums of money and ordering everybody about; and that trivial and impulsive charity is in some way contemptible. As Mr. Blatchford says, "The world does not want piety, but soap—and Socialism." Piety is one of the popular virtues, whereas soap and Socialism are two hobbies of the upper middle class.

These "healthy" ideals, as they are called, which our politicians and schoolmasters have borrowed from the aristocratic schools and applied to the democratic are by no means particularly appropriate to an impoverished democracy. A vague admiration for organised government and a vague distrust of individual aid cannot be made to fit in at all into the lives of people among whom kindness means lending a saucepan and honour means keeping out of the workhouse. It resolves itself either into discouraging that system of prompt and patchwork generosity which is a daily glory of the poor, or else into hazy advice to people who have no money not to give it recklessly away. Nor is the exaggerated glory of athletics, defensible enough in dealing with the rich who, if they did not romp and race, would eat and drink unwholesomely, by any means so much to the point when applied to people, most of whom will take a great deal of exercise anyhow, with spade or hammer, pickaxe or saw. And for the third case, of washing, it is obvious that the same sort of rhetoric about corporeal daintiness which is proper to an ornamental class cannot, merely as it stands, be applicable to a dustman. A gentleman is expected to be substantially spotless all the time. But it is no more discreditable for a scavenger to be dirty than for a deep-sea diver to be wet. A sweep is no more disgraced when he is covered with soot than Michael Angelo when he is covered with clay or Bayard when he is covered with blood. Nor have these extenders of the public school tradition done or suggested anything by way of a substitute for the present snobbish system which makes cleanliness almost impossible to the poor; I mean the general ritual of linen and the wearing of the cast-off clothes of the rich. One man moves into another man's clothes as he moves into another man's house. No wonder that our educationists are not horrified at a man picking up the aristocrat's second-hand trousers, when they themselves have only taken up the aristocrat's second-hand ideas.

Chapter Thirteen

THE OUTLAWED PARENT

THERE is one thing at least of which there is never so much as a whisper inside the popular schools; and that is the opinion of the people. The only persons who seem to have nothing to do with the education of the children are the parents. Yet the English poor have very definite traditions in many ways. They are hidden under embarrassment and irony; and those psychologists who have disentangled them talk of them as very strange, barbaric and secretive things. But, as a matter of fact, the traditions of the poor are mostly simply the traditions of humanity, a thing which many of us have not seen for some time. For instance, working men have a tradition that if one is talking about a vile thing it is better to talk of it in coarse language; one is the less likely to be seduced into excusing it. But mankind had this tradition also, until the Puritans and their children, the Ibsenites, started the opposite idea, that it does not matter what you say so long as you say it with long words and a long face. Or again, the educated classes have tabooed most jesting about personal appearance; but in doing this they taboo not only the humour of the slums but more than half the healthy literature of the world; they put polite nose-bags on the

noses of Punch and Bardolph, Stiggins and Cyrano de Ber-
gerac. Again, the educated classes have adopted a hideous
and heathen custom of considering death as too dreadful
to talk about, and letting it remain a secret for each person,
like some private malformation. The poor, on the contrary,
make a great gossip and display about bereavement; and
they are right. They have hold of a truth of psychology which
is at the back of all the funeral customs of the children of
men. The way to lessen sorrow is to make a lot of it. The
way to endure a painful crisis is to insist very much that it is
a crisis; to permit people who must feel sad at least to feel
important. In this the poor are simply the priests of the universal civilisation; and in their stuffy feasts and solemn chat-
tering there is the smell of the baked meats of Hamlet and
the dust and echo of the funeral games of Patroclus.

The things philanthropists barely excuse (or do not excuse)
in the life of the labouring classes are simply the things we
have to excuse in all the greatest monuments of man. It
may be that the labourer is as gross as Shakespeare or as
garrulous as Homer; that if he is religious he talks nearly as
much about hell as Dante; that if he is worldly he talks
nearly as much about drink as Dickens. Nor is the poor man
without historic support if he thinks less of that ceremonial
washing which Christ dismissed, and rather more of that
ceremonial drinking which Christ specially sanctified. The
only difference between the poor man of to-day and the
saints and heroes of history is that which in all classes sepa-
rates the common man who can feel things from the great
man who can express them. What he feels is merely the
heritage of man. Now nobody expects, of course, that the cab-
men and coal-heavers can be complete instructors of their
children any more than the squires and colonels and tea
merchants are complete instructors of their children. There

must be an educational specialist *in loco parentis*. But the master at Harrow is *in loco parentis;* the master in Hoxton is rather *contra parentem*. The vague politics of the squire, the vaguer virtues of the colonel, the soul and spiritual yearnings of a tea merchant are, in veritable practice, conveyed to the children of these people at the English public schools. But I wish here to ask a very plain and emphatic question. Can anyone alive even pretend to point out any way in which these special virtues and traditions of the poor are reproduced in the education of the poor? I do not wish the coster's irony to appear as coarsely in the school as it does in the taproom; but does it appear at all? Is the child taught to sympathise at all with his father's admirable cheerfulness and slang? I do not expect the pathetic, eager *pietas* of the mother, with her funeral clothes and funeral baked meats, to be exactly imitated in the educational system; but has it any influence at all on the educational system? Does any elementary schoolmaster accord it even an instant's consideration or respect? I do not expect the schoolmaster to hate hospitals and C.O.S. centres so much as the schoolboy's father; but does he hate them at all? Does he sympathise in the least with the poor man's point of honour against official institutions? Is it not quite certain that the ordinary elementary schoolmaster will think it not merely natural but simply conscientious to eradicate all these rugged legends of a laborious people, and on principle to preach soap and Socialism against beer and liberty? In the lower classes the schoolmaster does not work for the parent but against the parent. Modern education means handing down the customs of the minority, and rooting out the customs of the majority. Instead of their Christlike charity, their Shakespearean laughter and their high Homeric reverence for the dead, the poor have imposed on them mere pedantic copies of the prejudices of the remote rich. They must think a bathroom a necessity, because to the lucky it is a luxury; they must swing Swedish clubs, because their masters are afraid of English cudgels; and they must get over their prejudice against being fed by the parish, because aristocrats feel no shame about being fed by the nation.

Chapter Fourteen

FOLLY AND FEMALE EDUCATION

IT is the same in the case of girls. I am often solemnly asked what I think of the new ideas about female education. But there are no new ideas about female education. There is not, there never has been, even the vestige of a new idea. All the educational reformers did was to ask what was being done to boys and then go and do it to girls; just as they asked what was being taught to young squires and then taught it to young chimney-sweeps. What they call new ideas are very old ideas in the wrong place. Boys play football, why shouldn't girls play football; boys have school-colours, why shouldn't girls have school-colours; boys go in hundreds to day-schools; boys go to Oxford, why shouldn't girls go to Oxford—in short, boys grow moustaches, why shouldn't girls grow moustaches—that is about their notion of a new idea. There is no brain-work in the thing at all; no root query of what sex is, of whether it alters this or that, and why, any more than there is any imaginative grip of the humour and heart of the populace in the popular education. There is nothing but plodding, elaborate, elephantine imitation. And just as in the case of elementary teaching, the cases are of a cold and reckless inappropriateness. Even a savage could see that bodily things, at least, which are good for a man are very likely to be bad for a woman. Yet there is no boy's game, however brutal, which these mild lunatics have not promoted among girls. To take a stronger case, they give girls very heavy home-work; never reflecting that all girls have home-work already in their homes. It is all a part of the same silly subjugation; there must be a hard stick-up collar round the neck of a woman, because it is already a nuisance round the neck of a man. Though a Saxon serf, if he wore that collar of cardboard, would ask for his collar of brass.

It will then be answered, not without a sneer, "And what would you prefer? Would you go back to the elegant early Victorian female, with ringlets and smelling-bottle, doing a little in watercolours, dabbling a little in Italian, playing a little on the harp, writing in vulgar albums and painting on senseless screens? Do you prefer that?" To which I answer, "Emphatically, yes." I solidly prefer it to the new female education, for this reason, that I can see in it an intellectual design, while there is none in the other. I am by no means sure that even in point of practical fact that elegant female would not have been more than a match for most of the inelegant females. I fancy Jane Austen was stronger, sharper and shrewder than Charlotte Brontë; I am quite certain she was stronger, sharper and shrewder than George Eliot. She could do one thing neither of them could do, she could coolly and sensibly describe a man. I am not sure that the old great lady who could only smatter Italian was not more vigorous than the new great lady who can only stammer American; nor am I certain that the bygone duchesses who were scarcely successful when they painted Melrose Abbey, were so much more weak-minded than the modern duchesses who paint only their own faces, and are bad at that. But that is not the point. What was the theory, what was the idea, in their old, weak water-colours and their shaky Italian? The idea was the same which in a ruder rank expressed itself in homemade wines and hereditary recipes; and which, still, in a thousand unexpected ways, can be found clinging to the women of the poor. It was the idea I urged in the second part of this book: that the world must keep one great amateur, lest we all become artists and perish. Somebody must renounce all specialist conquests, that she may conquer all the conquerors. That she may be a queen of life, she must not be a private soldier in it. I do not think the elegant female with her bad Italian was a perfect product, any more than I think the slum woman talking gin and funerals is a perfect product; alas, there are few perfect products. But they come from a comprehensible idea; and the new woman comes from nothing and nowhere. It is right to have an ideal, it is right to have the right ideal, and these two have the right ideal. The slum mother with her funerals is the degenerate daughter of Antigone, the obstinate priestess of the household gods. The lady talking bad Italian was the decayed tenth cousin of Portia, the great and golden Italian lady, the Renascence amateur of life, who could be a barrister because she could be anything. Sunken and neglected in the sea of modern monotony and imitation, the types hold tightly to their original truths. Antigone, ugly, dirty and often drunken, will still bury her father. The elegant female, vapid and fading away to nothing, still feels faintly the fundamental difference between herself and her husband; that he must be Something in the City, that she may be everything in the country.

There was a time when you and I and all of us were all very close to God; so that even now the colour of a pebble (or a paint), the smell of a flower (or a firework) comes to our hearts with a kind of authority and certainty; as if they were fragments of a muddled message, or features of a forgotten face. To pour that fiery simplicity upon the whole of life is the only real aim of education; and closest to the child comes the woman—she understands. To say what she understands is beyond me; save only this, that it is not a solemnity. Rather it is a towering levity, an uproarious amateurishness of the universe, such as we felt when we were little and would as soon sing as garden, as soon paint as run. To smatter the tongues of men and angels, to dabble in the dreadful sciences, to juggle with pillars and pyramids and toss up the planets like balls, this is that inner audacity and indifference which the human soul, like a conjurer catching oranges, must keep up for ever. This is that insanely frivolous thing we call sanity. And the elegant female, drooping her ringlets over her water-colours, knew it and acted on it. She was juggling with frantic and flaming suns. She was maintaining the bold equilibrium of inferiorities which is the most mysterious of superiorities and perhaps the most unattainable. She was maintaining the prime truth of woman, the universal mother: that if a thing is worth doing, it is worth doing badly.

PART V.

THE HOME OF MAN

Chapter One

THE EMPIRE OF THE INSECT

A CULTIVATED Conservative friend of mine once exhibited great distress because in a gay moment I had called Edmund Burke an atheist. I need scarcely say that the remark lacked something of biographical precision; it was meant to. Burke was certainly not an atheist in his conscious cosmic theory, though he had not a special and flaming faith in God, like Robespierre. Nevertheless the remark had reference to a truth which it is here relevant to repeat. I mean that in the quarrel over the French Revolution Burke did stand for the atheistic attitude and mode of argument, as Robespierre stood for the theistic. The Revolution appealed to the idea of an abstract and eternal justice, beyond all local custom or convenience. If there are commands of God, then there must be rights of man. Here Burke made his brilliant diversion; he did not attack the Robespierre doctrine with the old mediæval doctrine of *jus divinum* which, like the Robespierre doctrine, was theistic), he attacked it with the modern argument of scientific relativity; in short, the argument of evolution. He suggested that humanity was everywhere moulded by or fitted to its environment and institutions; in fact, that each people practically got, not only the tyrant it deserved, but the tyrant that it ought to have. "I know nothing of the rights of men," he said, "but I know something of the rights of Englishmen." There you have the essential atheist. His argument is that we have got some protection by natural accident and growth; and why should we profess to think beyond it, for all the world as if we were the images of God! We are born under a House of Lords, as birds under a house of leaves; we live under a monarchy, as Negroes live under a tropic sun; it is not their fault if they are slaves, and it is not ours if we are snobs. Thus, long before Darwin struck his great blow at democracy, the essential of the Darwinian argument had been already urged against the French Revolution. Man, said Burke in effect, must adapt himself to everything, like an animal; he must not try to alter everything, like an angel. The last weak cry of the pious, pretty, half-artificial optimism and deism of the eighteenth century came in the voice of Sterne, saying, "God tempers the wind to the shorn lamb." And Burke, the iron evolutionist, essentially answered, "No; God tempers the shorn lamb to the wind." It is the lamb that has to adapt himself. That is, he either dies or becomes a particular kind of lamb who likes standing in a draught.

The sub-conscious popular instinct against Darwinism was not a mere offence at the grotesque notion of visiting one's grandfather in a cage in the Regent's Park. Men go in for drink, practical jokes and many other grotesque things; they do not much mind making beasts of themselves, and would not much mind having beasts made of their forefathers. The real instinct was much deeper and much more valuable. It was this: that when once one begins to think of man as a shifting and alterable thing, it is always easy for the strong and crafty to twist him into new shapes for all kinds of unnatural purposes. The popular instinct sees in such develop-

ments the possibility of backs bowed and hunch-backed
for their burden, or limbs twisted for their task. It has a very
well-grounded guess that whatever is done swiftly and systematically will mostly be done by a successful class and
almost solely in their interests. It has therefore a vision of
inhuman hybrids and half-human experiments much in the
style of Mr. Wells's "Island of Dr. Moreau." The rich man
may come to breeding a tribe of dwarfs to be his jockeys,
and a tribe of giants to be his hall-porters. Grooms might be
born bow-legged and tailors born cross-legged; perfumers
might have long, large noses and a crouching attitude, like
hounds of scent; and professional wine-tasters might have
the horrible expression of one tasting wine stamped upon
their faces as infants. Whatever wild image one employs it
cannot keep pace with the panic of the human fancy, when
once it supposes that the fixed type called man could be
changed. If some millionaire wanted arms, some porter must
grow ten arms like an octopus; if he wants legs, some mes-
senger-boy must go with a hundred trotting legs like a centipede. In the distorted mirror of hypothesis, that is, of the
unknown, men can dimly see such monstrous and evil
shapes; men run all to eye, or all to fingers, with nothing left
but one nostril or one ear. That is the nightmare with which
the mere notion of adaptation threatens us. That is the
nightmare that is not so very far from the reality.

It will be said that not the wildest evolutionist really asks
that we should become in any way unhuman or copy any
other animal. Pardon me, that is exactly what not merely the
wildest evolutionists urge, but some of the tamest evolutionists too. There has risen high in recent history an important
cultus which bids fair to be the religion of the future—which
means the religion of those few weak-minded people who
live in the future. It is typical of our time that it has to look

for its god through a microscope; and our time has marked a definite adoration of the insect. Like most things we call new, of course, it is not at all new as an idea; it is only new as an idolatry. Virgil takes bees seriously, but I doubt if he would have kept bees as carefully as he wrote about them. The wise king told the sluggard to watch the ant, a charming occupation—for a sluggard. But in our own time has appeared a very different tone, and more than one great man as well as numberless intelligent men have seriously suggested that we should study the insect because we are his inferiors. The old moralists merely took the virtues of man and distributed them quite decoratively and arbitrarily among the animals. The ant was an almost heraldic symbol of industry, as the lion was of courage or, for the matter of that, the pelican of charity. But if the mediævals had been convinced that a lion was not courageous, they would have dropped the lion and kept the courage; if the pelican is not charitable, they would say, so much the worse for the pelican. The old moralists, I say, permitted the ant to enforce and typify man's morality; they never allowed the ant to upset it. They used the ant for industry as the lark for punctuality; they looked up at the flapping birds and down at the crawling insects for a homely lesson. But we have lived to see a sect that does not look down at the insects, but looks up at the insects; that asks us essentially to bow down and worship beetles, like the ancient Egyptians.

Maurice Maeterlinck is a man of unmistakable genius, and genius always carries a magnifying glass. In the terrible crystal of his lens we have seen the bees not as a little yellow swarm, but rather in golden armies and hierarchies of warriors and queens. Imagination perpetually peers and creeps further down the avenues and vistas in the tubes of science, and one fancies every frantic reversal of proportions; the earwig striding across the echoing plain like an elephant, or the grasshopper coming roaring above our roofs like a vast aeroplane, as he leaps from Hertfordshire to Surrey. One seems to enter in a dream a temple of enormous entomology, whose architecture is based on something wilder than arms or backbones; in which the ribbed columns have the half-crawling look of dim and monstrous caterpillars, or the dome is a starry spider hung horribly in the void. There is one of the modern works of engineering that gives one something of this nameless fear of the exaggerations of an underworld; and that is the curious curved architecture of the underground railway, commonly called the Twopenny Tube. Those squat archways, without any upright line or pillar, look as if they had been tunnelled by huge worms who have never learned to lift their heads. It is the very underground Palace of the Serpent, the spirit of changing shape and colour, that is the enemy of man.

But it is not merely by such strange æsthetic suggestions that writers like Maeterlinck have influenced us in the matter; there is also an ethical side to the business. The upshot of M. Maeterlinck's book on bees is an admiration, one might also say an envy, of their collective spirituality; of the fact that they live only for something which is called the Soul of the Hive. And this admiration for the communal morality of insects is expressed in many other modern writers in various quarters and shapes; in Mr. Benjamin Kidd's theory of living only for the evolutionary future of our race, and in the great interest of some Socialists in ants, which they generally prefer to bees, I suppose, because they are not so brightly coloured. Not least among the hundred evidences of this vague insectolatry are the floods of flattery poured by modern people on that energetic nation of the Far East of which it has been said that "Patriotism is its only religion";

or in other words, that it lives only for the Soul of the Hive. When at long intervals of the centuries Christendom grows weak, morbid or sceptical, and mysterious Asia begins to move against us her dim populations and to pour them westward like·a dark movement of matter, in such cases it has been very common to compare the invasion to a plague of lice or incessant armies of locusts. The Eastern armies were indeed like insects; in their blind, busy destructiveness, in their black nihilism of personal outlook, in their hateful indifference to individual life and love, in their base belief in mere numbers, in their pessimistic courage and their atheistic patriotism, the riders and raiders of the East are indeed like all the creeping things of the earth. But never before, I think, have Christians called a Turk a locust and meant it as a compliment. Now for the first time we worship as well as fear; and trace with adoration that enormous form advancing vast and vague out of Asia, faintly discernible amid the mystic clouds of winged creatures hung over the wasted lands, thronging the skies like thunder and discolouring the skies like rain: Beelzebub, the Lord of Flies.

In resisting this horrible theory of the Soul of the Hive, we of Christendom stand not for ourselves, but for all humanity; for the essential and distinctive human idea, that one good and happy man is an end in himself, that a soul is worth saving. Nay, for those who like such biological fancies it might well be said that we stand as chiefs and champions of a whole section of nature, princes of the house whose cognisance is the backbone, standing for the milk of the individual mother and the courage of the wandering cub, representing the pathetic chivalry of the dog, the humour and perversity of cats, the affection of the tranquil horse, the loneliness of the lion. It is more to the point, however, to urge that this mere glorification of society as it is in the social insects, is a transformation and a dissolution in one of the outlines which have been specially the symbols of man. In the cloud and confusion of the flies and bees is growing fainter and fainter, as if finally disappearing, the idea of the human family. The hive has become larger than the house, the bees are destroying their captors; what the locust hath left the caterpillar hath eaten; and the little house and garden of our friend Jones is in a bad way.

Chapter Two

THE FALLACY OF THE UMBRELLA
STAND

When Lord Morley said that the House of Lords must be either mended or ended, he used a phrase which has caused some confusion; because it might seem to suggest that mending and ending are somewhat similar things. I wish specially to insist on the fact that mending and ending are opposite things. You mend a thing because you like it; you end a thing because you don't. To mend is to strengthen. I, for instance, disbelieve in oligarchy; so I would no more mend the House of Lords than I would mend a thumb-screw. On the other hand, I do believe in the family; therefore I would mend the family as I would mend a chair; and I will never deny for a moment that the modern family is a chair that wants mending. But here comes in the essential point about the mass of modern advanced sociologists. Here are two institutions that have always been fundamental with mankind, the family and the state. Anarchists, I believe, disbelieve in both. It is quite unfair to say that Socialists believe in the state, but do not believe in the family; thousands of Socialists believe more in the family than any Tory. But it is true to say that while Anarchists would end both, Socialists are specially engaged in mending (that is, strengthening and renewing) the state; and they are not specially engaged in strengthening and renewing the family They are not doing anything to define the functions of father, mother, and child, as such; they are not tightening the machine up again; they are not blackening in again the fading lines of the old drawing. With the state they are doing this: they are sharpening its machinery, they are blacking in its black dogmatic lines, they are making mere government in every way stronger and in some ways harsher than before. While they leave the home in ruins, they restore the hive, especially the stings. Indeed, some schemes of Labour and Poor Law reform recently advanced by distinguished Socialists, amount to little more than putting the largest number of people in the despotic power of Mr. Bumble. Apparently progress means being moved on—by the police.

The point it is my purpose to urge might perhaps be suggested thus: that Socialists and most social reformers of their colour are vividly conscious of the line between the kind of things that belong to the state and the kind of things that belong to mere chaos or uncoercible nature; they may force children to go to school before the sun rises, but they will not try to force the sun to rise; they will not, like Canute, banish the sea, but only the sea-bathers. But inside the outline of the state their lines are confused, and entities melt into each other. They have no firm instinctive sense of one thing being in its nature private and another public, of one thing being necessarily bond and another free. That is why piece by piece and quite silently, personal liberty is being stolen from Englishmen, as personal land has been silently stolen ever since the sixteenth century.

I can only put it sufficiently curtly in a careless simile. A Socialist means a man who thinks a walking-stick like an umbrella because they both go into the umbrella-stand. Yet they are as different as a battle-axe and a boot-jack. The essential idea of an umbrella is breadth and protection. The essential idea of a stick is slenderness and, partly, attack. The stick is the sword, the umbrella is the shield, but it is a shield against another and more nameless enemy—the hostile but anonymous universe. More properly, therefore, the umbrella is the roof; it is a kind of collapsible house. But the vital difference goes far deeper than this; it branches off into two kingdoms of man's mind, with a chasm between. For the point is this, that the umbrella is a shield against an enemy so actual as to be a mere nuisance; whereas the stick is a sword against enemies so entirely imaginary as to be a pure pleasure. The stick is not merely a sword, but a court sword; it is a thing of purely ceremonial swagger. One cannot express the emotion in any way except by saying that a man feels more like a man with a stick in his hand, just as he feels more like a man with a sword at his side. But nobody ever had any swelling sentiments about an umbrella; it is a convenience, like a doorscraper. An umbrella is a necessary evil. A walking-stick is a quite unnecessary good. This, I fancy, is the real explanation of the perpetual losing of umbrellas; one does not hear of people losing walking-sticks. For a walking-stick is a pleasure, a piece of real personal property; it is missed even when it is not needed. When my right hand forgets its stick may it forget its cunning. But anybody may forget an umbrella, as anybody might forget a shed that he had stood up in out of the rain. Anybody can forget a necessary thing.

If I might pursue the figure of speech, I might briefly say that the whole Collectivist error consists in saying that because two men can share an umbrella therefore two men can share a walking-stick. Umbrellas might possibly be replaced by some kind of common awnings covering certain streets from particular showers. But there is nothing but nonsense in the notion of swinging a communal stick; it is as if one spoke of twirling a communal moustache. It will be said that this is a frank fantasia and that no sociologists suggest such follies. Pardon me, they do. I will give a precise parallel to the case of the confusion of sticks and umbrellas, a parallel from a perpetually reiterated suggestion of reform. At least sixty Socialists out of a hundred, when they have spoken of common laundries, will go on at once to speak of common kitchens. This is just as mechanical and unintelligent as the fanciful case I have quoted. Sticks and umbrellas are both stiff rods that go into holes in a stand in the hall. Kitchens and washhouses are both large rooms full of heat and damp and steam. But the soul and function of the two things is utterly opposite. There is only one way of washing a shirt; that is, there is only one right way. There is no taste and fancy in tattered shirts. Nobody says, "Tomkins likes five holes in his shirt, but I must say, give me the good old four holes." Nobody says, "This washerwoman rips up the left leg of my pyjamas; now if there is one thing I insist on it is the *right* leg ripped up." The ideal washing is simply to send a thing back washed. But it is by no means true that the ideal cooking is simply to send a thing back cooked. Cooking is an art; it has in it personality and even perversity, for the definition of an art is that which must be personal and may be perverse. I know a man, not otherwise dainty, who cannot touch common sausages unless they are almost burnt to a coal. He wants his sausages fried to rags, yet he does not insist on his shirts being boiled to rags. I do not say that such points of culinary delicacy are of high importance. I do not say that the communal ideal must give way to them. What I say is that the communal ideal is not conscious of their existence, and therefore goes wrong from the very start, mixing a wholly public thing with a highly individual one. Perhaps we ought to accept communal kitchens in the social crisis, just as we should accept communal catsmeat in a siege. But the cultured Socialist, quite at his ease, by no means in a siege, talks about communal kitchens as if they were the same kind of things as communal laundries. This shows at the start that he misunderstands human nature. They are as different as three men singing the same chorus from three men playing three tunes on the same piano.

Chapter Three

THE DREADFUL DUTY OF GUDGE

In the quarrel earlier alluded to between the energetic Progressive and the obstinate Conservative (or, to talk a tenderer language, between Hudge and Gudge) the state of cross-purposes is at the present moment acute. The Tory says he wants to preserve family life in Cindertown; the Socialist very reasonably points out to him that in Cindertown at present there isn't any family life to preserve. But Hudge, the Socialist, in his turn is highly vague and mysterious about whether he would preserve the family life if there were any; or whether he will try to restore it where it has disappeared. It is all very confusing. The Tory sometimes talks as if he wanted to tighten the domestic bonds that do not exist; the Socialist as if he wanted to loosen the bonds that do not bind anybody. The question we all want to ask of both of them is the original ideal question, "Do you want to keep the family at all?" If Hudge, the Socialist, does want the family he must be prepared for the natural restraints, distinctions and divisions of labour in the family. He must brace himself up to bear the idea of the woman having a preference for the private house and a man for the public house. He must manage to endure somehow the idea

207

of a woman being womanly, which does not mean soft and yielding, but handy, thrifty, rather hard, and very humorous. He must confront without a quiver the notion of a child who shall be childish, that is, full of energy, but without an idea of independence; fundamentally as eager for authority as for information and butter-scotch. If a man, a woman and a child live together any more in free and sovereign households, these ancient relations will recur; and Hudge must put up with it. He can only avoid it by destroying the family, driving both sexes into sexless hives and hordes, and bringing up all children as the children of the State—like Oliver Twist. But if these stern words must be addressed to Hudge, neither shall Gudge escape a somewhat severe admonition. For the plain truth to be told pretty sharply to the Tory is this, that if *he* wants the family to remain, if he wants it to be strong enough to resist the rending forces of our essentially savage commerce, he must make some very big sacrifices and try to equalise property. The overwhelming mass of the English people at this particular instant are simply too poor to be domestic. They are as domestic as they can manage, they are much more domestic than the governing class; but they cannot get what good there was originally meant to be in this institution, simply because they have not got enough money. The man ought to stand for a certain magnanimity, quite lawfully expressed in throwing money away; but if under given circumstances he can only do it by throwing the week's food away, then he is not magnanimous but mean. The woman ought to stand for a certain wisdom which is well expressed in valuing things rightly and guarding money sensibly; but how is she to guard money if there is no money to guard? The child ought to look on his mother as a fountain of natural fun and poetry; but how can he unless the fountain, like other fountains, is allowed to play? What chance have any of these ancient arts and functions in a house so hideously topsy-turvy; a house where the woman is out working and the man isn't; and the child is forced by law to think his schoolmaster's requirements more important than his mother's? No, Gudge and his friends in the House of Lords and the Carlton Club must make up their minds on this matter and that very quickly. If they are content to have England turned into a beehive and an ant-hill, decorated here and there with a few faded butterflies playing at an old game called domesticity in the intervals of the divorce court, then let them have their empire of insects; they will find plenty of Socialists who will give it to them. But if they want a domestic England, they must "shell out," as the phrase goes, to a vastly greater extent than any Radical politician has yet dared to suggest; they must endure burdens much heavier than the Budget and strokes much deadlier than the death duties; for the thing to be done is nothing more nor less than the distribution of the great fortunes and the great estates. We can now only avoid Socialism by a change as vast as Socialism. If we are to save property we must distribute property, almost as sternly and sweepingly as did the French Revolution. If we are to preserve the family we must revolutionise the nation.

Chapter Four

A DOUBT

And now, as this book is drawing to a close, I will whisper in the reader's ear a horrible suspicion that has sometimes haunted me: the suspicion that Hudge and Gudge are secretly in partnership; that the quarrel they keep up in public is very much of a put-up job; and that the way in which they perpetually play into each other's hands is not an everlasting coincidence. Gudge, the plutocrat, wants an anarchic industrialism; Hudge, the idealist, provides him with lyric praises of anarchy. Gudge wants women-workers because they are cheaper; Hudge calls the woman's work "freedom to live her own life." Gudge wants steady and obedient workmen; Hudge preaches teetotalism—to workmen, not to Gudge. Gudge wants a tame and timid population who will never take arms against tyranny; Hudge proves from Tolstoy that nobody must take arms against anything. Gudge is naturally a healthy and well-washed gentleman; Hudge earnestly preaches the perfection of Gudge's washing to people who can't practise it. Above all, Gudge rules by a coarse and cruel system of sacking and sweating and bi-sexual toil which is totally inconsistent with the free family and which is bound to destroy it; therefore Hudge, stretching out his arms to the universe with a prophetic smile, tells us that the family is something that we shall soon gloriously outgrow.

I do not know whether the partnership of Hudge and Gudge is conscious or unconscious. I only know that between them they still keep the common man homeless. I only know I still meet Jones walking the streets in the grey twilight, looking sadly at the poles and barriers and low red goblin lanterns which still guard the house which is none the less his because he has never been in it.

Chapter Five

CONCLUSION

Here, it may be said, my book ends just where it ought to begin. I have said that the strong centres of modern English property must swiftly or slowly be broken up, if even the idea of property is to remain among Englishmen. There are two ways in which it could be done, a cold administration by quite detached officials, which is called Collectivism, or a personal distribution, so as to produce what is called Peasant Proprietorship. I think the latter solution the finer and more fully human, because it makes each man (as somebody blamed somebody for saying of the Pope) a sort of small god. A man on his own turf tastes eternity or, in other words, will give ten minutes more work than is required. But I believe I am justified in shutting the door on this vista of argument, instead of opening it. For this book is not designed to prove the case for Peasant Proprietorship, but to prove the case against modern sages who turn reform to a routine. The whole of this book has been a rambling and elaborate urging of one purely ethical fact. And if by any chance it should happen that there are still some who do not quite see what that point is, I will end with one plain parable, which is none the worse for being also a fact.

A little while ago certain doctors and other persons permitted by modern law to dictate to their shabbier fellow-
citizens, sent out an order that all little girls should have
their hair cut short. I mean, of course, all little girls whose
parents were poor. Many very unhealthy habits are common among rich little girls, but it will be long before any
doctors interfere forcibly with them. Now, the case for this
particular interference was this, that the poor are pressed
down from above into such stinking and suffocating under-
worlds of squalor, that poor people must not be allowed to
have hair, because in their case it must mean lice in the
hair. Therefore, the doctors propose to abolish the hair. It
never seems to have occurred to them to abolish the lice. Yet
it could be done. As is common in most modern discussions
the unmentionable thing is the pivot of the whole discussion.
It is obvious to any Christian man (that is, to any man with a
free soul) that any coercion applied to a cabman's daughter
ought, if possible, to be applied to a Cabinet Minister's
daughter. I will not ask why the doctors do not, as a matter
of fact, apply their rule to a Cabinet Minister's daughter. I
will not ask, because I know. They do not because they dare
not. But what is the excuse they would urge, what is the
plausible argument they would use, for thus cutting and
clipping poor children and not rich? Their argument would
be that the disease is more likely to be in the hair of poor
people than of rich, and why? Because the poor children
are forced (against all the instincts of the highly domestic
working classes) to crowd together in close rooms under a
wildly inefficient system of public instruction; and because
in one out of the forty children there may be offence, and
why? Because the poor man is so ground down by the great
rents of the great ground landlords that his wife often has
to work as well as he. Therefore she has no time to look after

the children; therefore one in forty of them is dirty. Because the working man has these two persons on top of him, the landlord sitting (literally) on his stomach, and the schoolmaster sitting (literally) on his head, the working man must allow his little girl's hair, first to be neglected from poverty, next to be poisoned by promiscuity, and lastly to be abolished by hygiene. He, perhaps, was proud of his little girl's hair. But he does not count.

Upon this simple principle (or rather precedent) the sociological doctor drives gaily ahead. When a crapulous tyranny crushes men down into the dirt, so that their very hair is dirty, the scientific course is clear. It would be long and laborious to cut off the heads of the tyrants; it is easier to cut off the hair of the slaves. In the same way, if it should ever happen that poor children, screaming with tooth-ache, disturbed any schoolmaster or artistic gentleman, it would be easy to pull out all the teeth of the poor; if their nails were disgustingly dirty, their nails could be plucked out; if their noses were indecently blown, their noses could be cut off. The appearance of our humbler fellow-citizen could be quite strikingly simplified before we had done with him. But all this is not a bit wilder than the brute fact that a doctor can walk into the house of a free man, whose daughter's hair may be as clean as spring flowers, and order him to cut it off. It never seems to strike these people that the lesson of lice in the slums is the wrongness of slums, not the wrongness of hair. Hair is, to say the least of it, a rooted thing. Its enemy (like the other insects and Oriental armies of whom we have spoken) sweeps upon us but seldom. In truth it is only by eternal institutions like hair that we can test passing institutions like empires. If a door is so built as to knock a man's head off when he enters it, it is built wrong.

The mob can never rebel unless it is conservative, at least

enough to have conserved some reasons for rebelling. It is the most awful thought in all our anarchy, that most of the ancient blows struck for freedom would not be struck at all to-day, because of the obscuration of the clean, popular customs from which they came. The insult that brought down the hammer of Wat Tyler might now be called a medical examination. That which Virginius loathed and avenged as foul slavery might now be praised as free love. The cruel taunt of Foulon, "Let them eat grass," might now be represented as the dying cry of an idealistic vegetarian. Those great scissors of science that would snip off the curls of the poor little school children are ceaselessly snapping closer and closer to cut off all the corners and fringes of the arts and honours of the poor. Soon they will be twisting necks to suit clean collars, and hacking feet to fit new boots. It never seems to strike them that the body is more than raiment; that the Sabbath was made for man; that all institutions shall be judged and damned by whether they have fitted the normal flesh and spirit. It is the test of political sanity to keep your head. It is the test of artistic sanity to keep your hair on.

Now the whole parable and purpose of these last pages, and indeed of all these pages, is this: to assert that we must instantly begin all over again, and begin at the other end. I begin with a little girl's hair. That I know is a good thing at any rate. Whatever else is evil, the pride of a good mother in the beauty of her daughter is good. It is one of those adamantine tendernesses which are the touchstones of every age and race. If other things are against it, other things must go down. If landlords and laws and sciences are against it, landlords and laws and sciences must go down. With the red hair of one she-urchin in the gutter I will set fire to all modern civilisation. Because a girl should have long hair,

she should have clean hair; because she should have clean
hair, she should not have an unclean home; because she
should not have an unclean home, she should have a free
and leisured mother; because she should have a free mother,
she should not have an usurious landlord; because there
should not be an usurious landlord, there should be a re-
distribution of property; because there should be a redistri-
bution of property, there shall be a revolution. That little
urchin with the gold-red hair (whom I have just watched
toddling past my house), she shall not be lopped and lamed
and altered; her hair shall not be cut short like a convict's.
No, all the kingdoms of the earth shall be hacked about
and mutilated to suit her. The winds of the world shall be
tempered to that lamb unshorn. All crowns that cannot fit
her head shall be broken; all raiment and building that
does not harmonise with her glory shall waste away. Her
mother may bid her bind her hair, for that is a natural authority; but the Emperor of the Planet shall not bid her to
cut it off. She is the human and sacred image; all around
her the social fabric shall sway and split and fall; the pillars
of society shall be shaken, and the roofs of ages come rush-
ing down; and not one hair of her head shall be harmed.